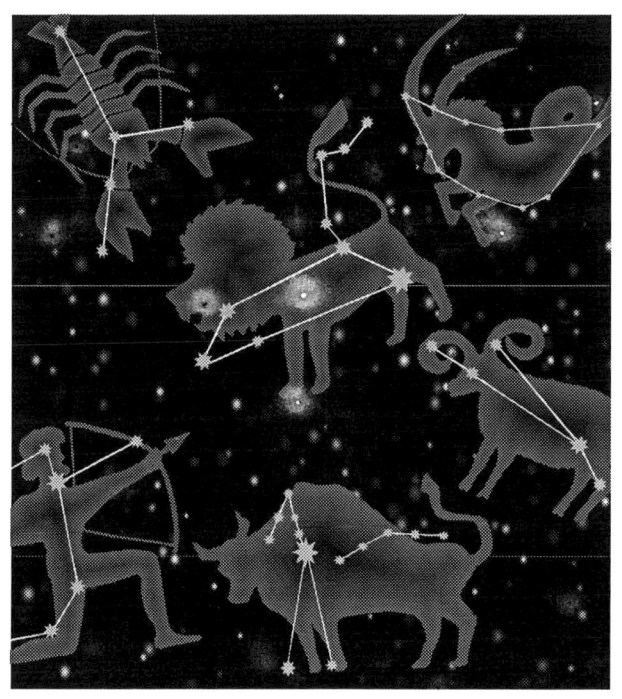

ZODIAC

CAMBRIDGESHIRE

Edited by Lynsey Hawkins

First published in Great Britain in 2002 by
YOUNG WRITERS
Remus House,
Coltsfoot Drive,
Peterborough, PE2 9JX
Telephone (01733) 890066

All Rights Reserved

Copyright Contributors 2002

HB ISBN 0 75433 566 6
SB ISBN 0 75433 567 4

FOREWORD

Young Writers was established in 1991 with the aim of promoting creative writing in children, to make reading and writing poetry fun.

Once again, this year proved to be a tremendous success with over 41,000 entries received nationwide.

The Zodiac competition has shown us the high standard of work and effort that children are capable of today. The competition has given us a vivid insight into the thoughts and experiences of today's younger generation. It is a reflection of the enthusiasm and creativity that teachers have injected into their pupils, and it shines clearly within this anthology.

The task of selecting poems was a difficult one, but nevertheless, an enjoyable experience. We hope you are as pleased with the final selection in *Zodiac Cambridgeshire* as we are.

Contents

Karl Tanner	1

Chesterton Community College

Charlotte Goode	1
Toby Clements	2
Celia Hipkin-Chastagnol	3
Katey Bell	4
Lee Langford	4
Andrew Gothard	5

Cottenham Village College

Patricia Hodapp	6
Fiona Milway	7

Cromwell Community College

Kieran Owen	8
Steven Daplyn	8
Francesca Clarke	9
Sarah Spendelow	9
Nick Woodard	9
Lee Benbow	10
Jamie McCleary	11
Daniel Rodgers	11
Amy Upton	12
Gemma Smith	12
Matthew Grainger	13
Allie Jones	13
Scott Twinn	14
Adrian Beeby	14
Aimee Bayliss	15
Joshua Harding	15
Cheryl Hall	16
Charlotte Dalliday	16
Nicole Spiers	16
Cindy Ponder	17
Luke Busby	17

Simon Howard	17
Abbey Baxter	18
Darren Sharpe	18
Oliver Harlock	18
Chelsey Gill	19
Leigh Clarke	19
Dominic Hayward	19
Laura Dennis	20
Kerry Hampson	20
Daniel MacKenzie	21
Verity Roscoe	21
Patrick Hayden	22
Sarah Reid	22
Victoria Salisbury	23
Bethany Hitch	23
Rachel Fyson	24
Rebekah Gill	24
Oliver Canham	25
Luke French	26
Zara Perkins	26
Adam Brewster	27
Harrison Salter	27
Bryel Parnell	28
Dawn Gleaves	28
Julie Heading	29
Thomas Salisbury	29
Freya Robinson	30
Keeley Hardman	30
Michelle Smalley	31
Charlotte Roberts	31
Laura Allen	32
Stephen Reed	32
Victoria Weatherby	33
Lloyd White	33
Helen Pitkin	33
Steven Reid	34
Karl Tanner	34
Grace Housley-Stott	35

Samantha Rex	35
Kathlene Cavilla	36
Natalie Rayner	36
Kirsty Farrington	37
Lisa Nicholas	37
Jonathan Clarke	38
Matthew Smith	38
Lewis Aitcheson	39
Amy Lince	39
Zoe Peverill	40
Laura Edgley	40
Hollie Wootton	41
Emma Watkins	42
Sarah Jane Snow	42
Zoe Feast	43
Ryan Gibson	44
John Cole	45
Sophie English	45
Lucy White	46
Craig Barnes	46
Tanith Hayward	47
Vicky Bannister	47
Stephanie Boyden	48
John Gleaves	49
Kelly Burrows	50
Matthew Lacey	50

Manor Community College

Marcus Clarke	50
Natalie Edwards	51
Felicity Price	51
Michael Kember	52
Emily Hall	52
Jamie Thomas	52
Sarah Watson	53
Jake Rowland	53
Rochelle Ebanks	54
Kieran Delph	54

    Katie Asby   55
    Hannah Mallows   55

Orton Longueville School
    Jenny Crawford   56

Oundle & Laxton Schools
    Robin Smid   57
    Kate Mason   58
    Katherine Bullard   59
    Amy Shaw   60
    Hannah Matthews   61
    Khadija Kachra   62
    Huw Dawson   62
    Amila Subramaniam   63
    Shanna Martens   64
    Harriet Scriven   65
    Alice McDonald   66
    Rosalie Brooman-White   67

St Bede's School, Cambridge
    Victoria Bonnici   68
    Jessica Marsh   68
    Nick Lamble   69
    Deborah Few   70
    Zoe Cox   70
    Stacey Purath   71
    Jamie Simms   71
    Karl Walker   72
    Jemima Estabrook   72
    Hannah Megson   73
    Jack Scotney   73
    Rachel Moden   74
    Danielle Ball   74
    Anna Hornby   75
    Suzanne Patterson   75
    Scott Collen   76
    Claire Hancock   76

James Paterson	77
Anna McNamara	77
Louise Pigott	78
Becky Wright	78
Owen Sanderson	79
Elizabeth Cameron	80
Jasmin Mokarram	80
Joe Minervino	81
Naomi Cave	82
Maria Kaye	83
Jeanette Langford	84
Michael Niskin	85
Chris Allen	86
Sarah Nightingale	87
Philip Bateman	88
Rebecca Clarke	89
Sophie Lambert	90
Oliver Worth	91
Thomas Lovell	92
Claire Thompson	92
Rachel Lister	93
Heather Lee	94
Jessica Marshall	94
Holly Marshall	95
Stephanie Allum	96
Nikki Jackson	96
Steven Kylstra	97
Lindsay Brand	98
Chris Chapman	98
Rebecca Saunders	99
Richard Griffiths	100
Kyle Payne	100
Ruth Mullett	101
Charlotte Gutsell	101
Kimberley Muranyi	102
Alison Lygo	103
Alice Matthews	104
Morgan Howarth	104

Javan Hirst	105
Reuben Mashford	105
Claire Osbourn	106
Frances Hall	107
Jenny Warnes	108
Charlotte Randles-Mills	108
Jeremy Badley	109
Vanessa Hunt	110
Paul Johnson	110
Robert Jackson	111
Jennie Johnson	112
Benjamin Dixon	112
Tad Cook	113
Alistair Campbell	113
Christopher Thurston	114
Simon Pettit	114
Olivia Pinnock	115
Julian Dickson	116
Rachel Moseley	117
Holly Gowler	118

Sawston Village College

Ellis Winster	118
Joanne Farley	119
Rowena Smith-Lamkin	120
Melody Tomlin	120
Helen Wragg	121
Maria Reali	121
Max Appleton	122
Donielle Brymer	123
Megan Saunders	124
Susannah Bangham	125
Catherine Nobes	126
Sam Chequer & Chris Evans	126
Michael Ford	127
Lucy Deeming	127
Sophie Maloney	128
Peter Martin	128

Tom Chalk	129
Abigail Hunt	129
Fraser Clark	130
Charlie Collier	130
Natasha DeMartino	131
Lucy Baglin	132
Sarah Pettican	133
John Young	134
Bai-ou He	135
William Hewson	136
Adam Marritt	136
Laurence Nye	137
Alex Campbell	137
Harriet Richmond	138
Rebecca Pryce	139
Megan Overend	140
Emma Hewer	140
Hannah Margaret Edwards	141
Martin Ball	142
Danny Harris	142
Jenny Nobes	143
Chloé Pantazi	143
Alistair White	144
Johanna Yassin	145
Clare Tubby	146
Iain Hyde	146
Maya Bienz	147
Holly-Bethe Moseley	148
Dan Matthews	148
Hannah Kite	149
Eleanor Tubby	149
Lauren King	150
Stephanie Howe	150
Elizabeth Hale	151
Sarah Thompson	152
Jodi Keen	152
Freya Chaplin	153
Martyn Willis	153

Susannah Hodge	154
Emma Cracknell	155
Amber Dyer	156
Clare Woods	156
Patrick McCrae	157
Leon Cheng	157
Jasmine Phillips	158
Aron Murray	158
James Camp	159
Serena Flack	159
Charlotte Judd	160
Olivia Smith	160
Lucy Squire	161
Kelly Tombs	161
Lucinda Broad	162
Emily Brisley	163
Robert MacKenzie	164
Jessica Goody	164
Catarina Constância	165
Jamie Elston	166
Coba Vermaak	167
Samantha Rule	168
Craig Plater	168
Sarah Phillips	169
Nathaniel Nye	169

Soham Village College

Sinead Mathias	170
Dieuwertje Laker	171
Christopher Reed	172
Joshua Woodroffe	173
Isaac McGinley	174
Rachele Guggiari	174
Katie Rushforth	175
Kyle Mucha	176
Sarah Paines	176
Sarah Gillett	177
Ryan Crockford	178

	Craig Parnell	179
	Natasha Pulley	180
	Amy-Louise Rankin	181
	James Turner	182
	Jason Allen	182
	Meredith Thorpe	183
	Charlotte Woodbridge	184
	Frankie Houck	185
	Beth Fuller	186
	Harriet Wright	186
	Charlotte Avison	187
	Kimberley Ashwell	188
	Lucy Gray	188
	Amanda Pettit	189
	Helena Evans	190
	Shona Daly	191
	Oliver Williams	192
	Thomas Seljamae	192
	Sarah Bayes	193
	Tori Atkinson	194
	Caroline Watson	194
	Emma Badcock	195
	Rachel Peachey	196
	Alex Fogg	196
The Leys School		
	David Aylmer	197
	Madeleine Williams	198
	Adam Arnot Drummond	199
	Chris Colgate	200
	Kate O'Brien	201
	Laura Taylor	202
The Netherhall School		
	Carla Swift	202
	Fizza Mirza	203
	Lee Fowle	203
	Leanne Haden	204

Marc Brown	205
Charlotte Okten	205
Bilesh Ladva	206
Samantha Pearson	206
Amy McKechnie	207
Verity Shelbourne	207
Hitanshu Barot	207
Rachel Prat	208
Andrea-Claire Fordham	208
Amy Cook	209
Jade Gatt	209
Sarah Norman	210
Sarah Baron	210
Alistair Cray	211
Helen Proffitt	212
Oliver Oakman	212
Charley Atherton	213
Luke Latty	213
Ali Hammad	214
Rachel Philpott	214
Becky White	215
Yaa Acheampong	215
Catherine Darler	216
Oliver Francis	218
Hayley Burch	219
Liam Williamson	219
Lisa Randall	219
Flore Elisabeth Suter	220
Alice Miller	220
Jonathan Lander	221
Nesha Patel	222
Jodie Tucker	222
Charlotte Taylor	222
Denice Nowlan	223
Sarah Holmes	224
Andrew Flynn	224
Henry Stockley	225

Marianna Murray		225
Rachel Story		226

The Perse School For Girls
Veronica Andersson		226
Rachel Armitage		227
Eleanor Westgarth-Flynn		228
Victoria Ball		228
Susanna Bridge		229
Jessica Bull		230

The Poems

ARMY

People: Running from people, bang, bang!
Guns: Buzzing around on the floor.
Armies: Bang, bang onto the floor - dead.
Tanks: Fire, fire on the horses.
Sleeping: All day and no peace.

Karl Tanner (13)

LOVE

Love is such a powerful emotion,
All it needs is time and devotion
When your love is always on your mind,
He's funny, caring, loving and kind.
When all you need is a kiss and a cuddle
Your feelings are in one large muddle
Then when your love goes away
Your heart and mind have to pay
When you know the one you love will never love you
You're all choked up, you don't know what to do
When the feeling inside is different from before
All you can do is love them even more
When 'I love you' are the words you say
All they do is laugh and walk away
You see your love laughing and joking
You know they wouldn't save you if you were choking.
You can't help the way you feel inside,
'Cos all you want is your love by your side,
When the one you love
Is watching you from up above
All you can do is think and cry
Then say your one last goodbye.

Charlotte Goode (15)
Chesterton Community College

DAD, MUM AND ME

Dad works at the bakery,
Mum works at the train station,
I go to school.

Dad didn't come home,
Mum was angry,
I went to school.

Dad moved,
Mum was crying,
I went to school.

Dad came back,
Mum shouted,
I went to school.

Dad got angry,
Mum got hurt,
I went to school.

Dad shouted at me,
Mum helped me,
I went to school.

Dad left,
Mum was crying,
I went to school.

Dad's gone,
Mum's sad,
I went to school.

Gran looked after me,
Mum met Jack,
I went to school.

Gran's gone
Mum? Dad?
I stayed home.

Toby Clements (14)
Chesterton Community College

SILENT QUESTIONS

What do you say,
When you don't know the answer?
What do you do,
When you can't feel a thing?
Who do you cry for,
When tears are too few?
Why do you smile,
When you're weeping within?

Do you wish on a star,
When smoke fills the night?
Do you pretend not to know,
When to know is too much?
Do you shine like a light,
When the flame has grown dim?
Do you appear not to care,
When only crying seems right?

How many people,
See what I see?
How many people,
Feel just like me?
How will this end,
When you don't know the start?
What can I give?
Just a human heart.

Celia Hipkin-Chastagnol (14)
Chesterton Community College

AS I WALK BY

Many people laugh,
Many people cry,
   And me, I just smile as I walk by.
Some kid has broken a glass,
His mum says not to worry.
Some man has done some wrong,
And is trying to say sorry.
   And me, I just smile as I walk by.
Old people, new people, used people.
People who see someone they know,
Some go to say hello,
Others pretend they don't really know.
   And me, I just smile as I walk by.
A mother laden with shopping bags,
Trying to find her kids.
And a mad-looking tramp,
Trying to find his wits.
   And me, I just smile as I walk by.

And when I go, their lives will go on without me,
Some will find happiness, but all will die.
   And me, I just smile as I walk by.

Katey Bell (15)
Chesterton Community College

THE DIVINE INTERVENTION

Tangled in God's ravelled burning bush, I am suspended upside-down,
From my fragile, unconscious symphony to my ankle,
In pink and dark universe surrounded by an unknown realm.
I must soon reach the ears of this lion's den as a messenger.
Though right now my voice is too far to be seen.
My voice too distant to be heard.

The bleeding body is giving way.
Flaming words tear at the smooth flesh around me.
I try to climb the cavern of inferno to the high heavens
Only then does the line break.
I fall out of the sky's womb
Onto a land where I know nothing,
But die forgiving everything.

Lee Langford (16)
Chesterton Community College

MY DREAM ANIMAL

My dream is to be an elephant
Every second I step on an ant,
Spraying water out of my trunk
Seeing a mouse would make me do a bunk.

I might like to be a bear
With all that fuzzy, wuzzy hair.
With one swing of the paw
Catching plenty of fish, raw.

How about being a monkey?
That would be cool and funky
Swinging from vine to vine
Up, down and in a straight line.

Better than that -
I'd rather be a cat,
Chasing all those mice
Now that would be nice.

Now I've decided. Instead,
I would rather be myself, in bed.

Andrew Gothard (15)
Chesterton Community College

SEASONS IN MINNESOTA

Summer is a time of fun,
Children playing in the sun.
People laying on the beach,
Teachers do not have to teach.

River or lake is a good place to stay,
When on summer holiday.
Running, swimming, fishing, boating,
Biking, camping, reading, rowing.

When autumn comes and leaves fall down,
People gather in the town.
Harvest day is coming soon,
After that will be a full moon.

Thanksgiving's a huge feast every year,
Loads of food, perhaps maybe a deer.
Carrots and onions, rabbit and stew,
Chicken, apples and pumpkin pie too.

After that when winter winds blow,
Quiet descends, here comes the snow!
Fires built to keep things warm,
Hot chocolate served in the midst of the storm.

Old ones shiver while children skate,
Others ski and for spring they wait.
Santa Claus comes - oh what a joy!
He brings a gift to each girl and boy.

Spring is here! They all say
Ice and snow have melted away.
The seasons complete, a new year begun -
Soon will be time for summer fun!

Patricia Hodapp (12)
Cottenham Village College

NOT UNSPOKEN

Like a chestnut-coloured horse
In a mahogany room
As a velvety garment with rubies and jewels
If only for a burgundy moment
On a warm morello night
With a fragrance like claret
Like a basket of red roses
For a grandmother wearing a rusty-coloured vest
Or a child with carnations the colour of blood
Wearing scarlet hat and gloves and coat
Below a terracotta chimney row
Witnessed by a tall crimson door.
But the colours are fading for there is no love anymore.

Like a dark mare
In an ash-coated room
As the mysterious grey gown without rubies nor jewels
If for a sinful moment
On a cold, stormy night
With the taste of vengeance
Like a crown of thorns
For a master dressed in evil
Or a child caked in smut
Wearing shadowy hat and gloves and coat
Above a murky, musty street
Witnessed by a closed black door
Because the colour just isn't there anymore.

To find the colours, just look again
For in each person we find a new token
So find your love, my child, my dear
For the world is not unspoken.

Fiona Milway (11)
Cottenham Village College

Mars Sports Day

M artians might live on Mars
A ttacking lost spaceships
R iding space horses for sports day
S pace is big so don't explore it!

S wimming in molten rock
P addling in rocks,
O r
R iding space horses down the field
T aming wild space cows for aliens
S mirking if you cheat, you won't for long.

D rinking ice cream through your nostrils
A lovely day out, if you can call it that
Y elping if you get stuck in the inferno.

Kieran Owen (11)
Cromwell Community College

Football Crazy

F unny football is so cool
O ver a period of time
O ut with your mates
T elling jokes with the lads
B eing booked isn't so cool
A t least when you score a goal
L ovely goals make fans cheer
L ike David Beckham's this year!

Steven Daplyn (13)
Cromwell Community College

ZODIAC

Z ing through the sky a little, bright light
O n a planet hot and cold, when will we be going home
D own a black hole and you're gone
I magine being on a shooting star
A round the Earth and back again
C louds are white, like a bright light.

Francesca Clarke (13)
Cromwell Community College

ZODIAC

Z igzagging through the dark sky
O ver the moon
D iving over Neptune
I ncredible journey's begun
A s the stars shine brightly
C urling through the dark sky.

Sarah Spendelow (13)
Cromwell Community College

ZODIAC

Z is for zodiac signs
O is for observation with the stars
D is for the Big Dipper,
I is for the incredible sight,
A is for the animals of the zodiac,
C is for constellations of the sky.

Nick Woodard (13)
Cromwell Community College

PREDICTION OF THE WEEK

Leo:
This week in the star,
Jupiter and Mars are aligned on your side
Great riches shall you inherit
Nevertheless, beware of the rocky ride
Great dangers shall you encounter.

The reward isn't a sure thing,
For if you slip up
Danger bells will begin to ring.

Your pride shall be in trouble,
Your senses must call a truce,
For an evil creature is out there
The green-eyed monster is loose,
And if it grabs hold of you
The score shall be tied at deuce.

The final point is one of courage,
One, which could swing both ways.
For you to become the victor
Your omens must you slay.

You must trounce that green-eyed monster,
You must crush the sin of greed,
And if you can manage to do this
Of my one last warning please, take heed.

To find the key to your treasure,
To find your final reward . . .
Buy next week's issue for 99p,
You'll agree, easy to afford.

Lee Benbow (14)
Cromwell Community College

TEAR IN MY EYE

Do you know how hard it is to live without you?
So I have a tear in my eye because of you.

Do you know how much pain it is not living with your brother?
So I have a tear in my eye because of you.

Can I come home?
No!
Why, don't you love me?
Yes,
So why can't I come home?
Because you are at school
So I have a tear in my eye because of you.

Jamie McCleary (14)
Cromwell Community College

I TRIED, I TRIED

This rhyme is hard to make
But I tried.
Because I could not do this rhyme
I cried.
With all of this thinking
I'm going to go blind!
I am getting in a muddle
My fingers are getting tired.
Please don't scold me
I tried, I tried
And no one knows how hard it was to write this rhyme.

Daniel Rodgers (13)
Cromwell Community College

THE KING OF THE JUNGLE

The king of the jungle, waiting, watching,
Ready to pounce on the innocent animal
He jumps, animal howling and squealing
He flees
He leaves for the tree in the abandoned field
He sleeps, peaceful, quiet,
A noise is coming from the bushes
Rustle, rustle,
He opens one eye, he pounces,
Roaring viciously,
No more noise
He goes back to sleep, no noise, just the wind
Getting back energy for tomorrow.

Amy Upton (13)
Cromwell Community College

THE STARS

Look up to the sky
What do I see?
A thousand stars looking down at me
Big ones, small ones, making shapes,
This bunch look like a crowd of apes,
There's 1, 2, 3, 4, 5,
The sky at night is very much alive
What's happening now?
The stars are disappearing,
I know, a big, grey cloud is appearing.
The stars are gone and the day has come
Maybe tomorrow I'll again see them!

Gemma Smith (13)
Cromwell Community College

THE CHINESE ZODIAC

There are different animals in the Chinese zodiac
All different in their ways
The dog, the rat, the dragon,
All have something to say.
The dog is brave and clever
The rat is clever too
The dragon is strong and faithful
I wonder which one is you?
I personally am year of the snake
Sneaky, smart and playful
And all the people that I know
Can prove that I am faithful.

Matthew Grainger (12)
Cromwell Community College

EMOTIONS

Emotions are strange,
Emotions are personal,
Every different person's emotions are . . .
Love, hate, happiness and sadness.
Emotions are like the planets,
Cold like Pluto,
Her emotions are sad and unfortunate, all alone,
Not like the planet of war, Mars,
Her emotion is angry and confused.
Venus is surrounded in chemical clouds
She is wound in blue beauty
Her emotion is love.

Allie Jones (12)
Cromwell Community College

THE STARS

Stars are such wonderful things
Fantastic for the wishes they bring
The danger within
The old, rusty tin
Time is running out
Just don't shout.

An atom bomb explodes
Just hate it loads
For the places we want to go
For the places of dreams.

NASA, ESA have their fantasies
But the danger is still just . . .
Plain to see.

Scott Twinn (13)
Cromwell Community College

MY SONG

My song is little,
My song is quick,
Your gonna get to know it,
It's really wick'
I watch lotsa movies,
I like science fic'
Me mate's all soppy,
'E writes roman'ic.
I like me poems,
But I 'ate limerick'
I'm no good at school work,
Me mates say I'm fick!

Adrian Beeby (11)
Cromwell Community College

My Teachers At School

My English teacher, Mr Terry,
Taps his fingers on the table
Taps his fingers on the board
He can be funny
He's like this all hour long.

My maths teacher, Miss Rae,
She has sums going through her head all day
She sets two pieces of homework every week
She also taps on her blackboard.

Mr Parker is my form teacher
He's funny but he likes to shout
He likes to be proud of us too
Just like he is in the form photo.

Aimee Bayliss (11)
Cromwell Community College

The Josh Rap

Pencil cases brandishing,
Zips are a-flowing,
Disco divas dancing,
Boys all a-howling,
Kids taking the mick,
Teachers havin' a flip,
And out of the classroom they go
Hi ho, hi ho,
Pencil cases flying
Ryan Maytum crying,
And all the kids in Cromwell School
Are havin' a ball!

Joshua Harding (11)
Cromwell Community College

STARS

Stars in the sky are so bright
They are made up of different shapes
They are very tiny and small
Mind out! They are very hot.
You might even see a shooting star
They sparkle in the dark
Maybe there is none at all.

Cheryl Hall (14)
Cromwell Community College

STAR SIGNS

Capricorn, Pisces, Aries, Taurus,
Gemini, Cancer, Leo, Virgo, Libra,
Scorpio, Sagittarius, Aquarius
Now take your pick
Which one are you?
I am one and so are you!

Charlotte Dalliday (13)
Cromwell Community College

LOST IN SPACE

Once I was lost in space
And it was all black
And a few yellow dots
And it was dark
But it was beautiful
And then I found Earth.

Nicole Spiers (11)
Cromwell Community College

ZODIAC, GET REAL!

Z odiac, I mean who actually believes it?
O riginal, I grant them that,
D elivered in the paper, it makes my dad's day.
I was born in October, that makes me Libra,
A pparently that makes me balanced, I'm not.
C ourageous idea, but tell me who actually believes it|?

Cindy Ponder (12)
Cromwell Community College

ZODIAC

Z illions and zillions
O f stars
D otted all around the sky
I n a black, silky blanket
A black hole for anything and everything
C overed in a . . . black . . . silky . . . blanket.

Luke Busby (12)
Cromwell Community College

FARMERS

F arming is cool
A straw stack standing tall
R abbits running wild
M essing around in the yard
E verybody acting hard
R elatives coming to stay
S un shining as I sit on the hay.

Simon Howard (13)
Cromwell Community College

I Am A Gemini

I am a Gemini, that's a fact,
I love to laugh and mess about
I am a Gemini, it's true, it's true,
I am fantastic and so are you.
Me and my mate we're Gemini
Mad, cos our birthday's in May
And we're so glad.

Abbey Baxter (12)
Cromwell Community College

Space

I often wonder is there life up there
In the big, black mist called space?
Are there men on Mars?
Women on Venus?
Dogs on Pluto?

Darren Sharpe (13)
Cromwell Community College

The Roller Coaster

I rode the roller coaster
It gave me such a scare
I thought I saw my
Tummy, still floating in the air!

Oliver Harlock (13)
Cromwell Community College

STARS

So many pictures
Made up from the stars
Shining brightly in the sky
If you're scared of the dark
Look up at the stars
If you're lost and you can't find your way home
Find the North Star.

Chelsey Gill (11)
Cromwell Community College

WHY?

Why does my life seem so mean?
Everyone thinks I am so keen,
Why do I want to die?
What is wrong if you want to cry?
Why is my life so cruel?
Well, it isn't at all.

Leigh Clarke (13)
Cromwell Community College

THE RADIOACTIVE MAN FROM MARS

There was a man from Mars
Who went along and blew up some cars
The man was nuked,
He then puked,
And the vomit went up to the stars!

Dominic Hayward (13)
Cromwell Community College

STAR TREK

They say girls are from Venus,
And men are from Mars,
There may be life,
Out there in the stars.

Ugly aliens from different planets,
Or floating around in space,
Will they ever come and visit,
Our human race?

What would it be like to visit the moon,
Leave in March
And come back in June?

Do aliens live the same lives as us
Go to school, come home on the bus?
Will we ever knock on their door,
And boldly go where no man has gone before?

Laura Dennis (13)
Cromwell Community College

CUSTARD PIES

When you look at the sky at night,
All the stars glow at great height,
The constellations join up in the sky,
Sagittarius and Aquarius playing with custard pies,
Somebody's hiding behind Libra, oh its Gemini,
Taurus is chasing Cancer trying to poke Scorpio in the eye,
When lovers look at the sky wondering where is Aries,
Then they see he's playing with the fairies.

Kerry Hampson (15)
Cromwell Community College

HOPES AND DREAMS

Hopes are big,
Dreams are too,
Put them together and they equal life,
Life is massive, in fact it's huge.
So many things that we will never be able to do.

Dreams are life,
Everybody dreams of being at the top,
Not many of us reach the top for those who do,
It's a dream come true.

Hopes are a light at the end of a tunnel,
Everybody hopes that they will be the best at what they want to be.

Hopes are better than dreams
Because dreams sometimes don't come true,
But you can always hope!

Daniel MacKenzie (12)
Cromwell Community College

HORIZON

The horizon is always so far away
But also so close.
At sunrise the sun will blind you,
With light and colour of the sky.
At sunset the sun shall go
And bring darkness throughout the land
But as the sun goes down
The night-time stars come out,
And fill the skies with pictures.

Verity Roscoe (12)
Cromwell Community College

WWF

The WWF is cool.
Like a swimming pool.
Kurt Angle, Angle Slams like I've never saw
That's why he's my favourite superstar
The Undertaker lost rides
Like rocks getting hit by tides
Can you smell what The Rock is cooking!
Like Lita was looking.

Jeff Hardy, Swanton Bomb
He misses like usual
Matt Hardy, Twist of Fate
Will give Lita her date
And that's the end of Raw
Is war!

Patrick Hayden (11)
Cromwell Community College

THE MAN IN THE MOON

Now tell me, is there a man in the moon
Who has little houses made of cheese?
Does he sit there all night and watch us sleep
Then go away when the sun comes out
Because the sun melts the moon?
Is he the only one out there?
Are there aliens and UFOs?
And do they all sit there and eat cheese
While the sun's out?
So, can I ask you? Is there a man on the moon?
We will never know
Will we?

Sarah Reid (12)
Cromwell Community College

WHEN I AM A TEACHER

When I have grown older
And gone to college galore
I want to be a teacher
And have my name written on the door.
Saying 'Class 8, Mrs Salisbury,
Work hard and please don't talk.
For if you do not do it
I'll make you take a walk.'

No, I wouldn't, I'm joking
I would not be that bad
In fact if I'm honest
I would be totally mad!

I would have funky paper
Stuck up on my walls
And little trays for everything,
When I am a teacher!

Victoria Salisbury (11)
Cromwell Community College

WHAT ARE STARS?

As I sit down at night and look at the stars
I wonder what they really are
Are they little twinkling fairies up high
Or are they soldiers guarding the night sky?
Are they some sort of door
Or are they planets having a war?
They might be dreams that come from Mars
They might be little wishing stars . . .?

I don't know, do you?

Bethany Hitch (13)
Cromwell Community College

SCHOOL THINGS

Morning rises,
Ready for school,
Teaching children,
Educating them all.
Reading and speaking,
Rhythm and rhyme,
Yes I am ready for school, it's time.

French can be easy, French can be hard,
Reading and writing,
In the school yard.
End of the day,
Nearly home time,
Done all my homework,
So it's sleeping time.

School is fun
College is great,
Hoping to see,
Organisation indeed.
Oh, I could do with a rest,
Little brother is a pest.

Rachel Fyson (12)
Cromwell Community College

MY FRIEND THE ALIEN

My friend the alien,
Comes from far away,
He can see many things,
You don't see day by day.

My friend the alien,
Travels round the world
In his blue and red spaceship,
The legs are really curled.

My friend the alien,
Has eight fingers on each hand,
He can play lots of instruments
In his own one-man-band.

My friend the alien,
Went away one day,
He never came back,
So I don't know what to say!

Rebekah Gill (12)
Cromwell Community College

THE GRAVEYARD

The rustling of leaves and
An eerie howl of the wind,
Like a pack of wolves.

Hoots of owls in the trees
A loud crack of lightning
The full moon on a cloudless night
Projecting scary pictures on the trees.

Rattling chains around the graves
A black, shadowy figure
The figure is holding a bloody scythe
He'll cut your head straight off.

You're dead too
Blood is everywhere and it flickers like a stream
From your severed body . . .

. . . you are one of them now!

Oliver Canham (13)
Cromwell Community College

The Planets

There are lots of different planets,
All lined up in a row.
Each and every one is special,
As everyone should know.

There's Mercury, Venus, Earth,
Saturn, Jupiter and Mars
The red planet's raging with anger,
But that's completely different to ours.

Our planet is full of life,
We will keep the others at bay.
My family is here and I have to announce,
That I am here to stay.

Luke French (12)
Cromwell Community College

The Shark

The shark is a prowler
At the bottom of the sea
It looks for prey,
A fish swims by
It enters a chase that
It will not win,
In the frightening, murky sea,
In a puff of sand,
In one second,
The fish is gone
The shark is smiling as he moves on.

Zara Perkins
Cromwell Community College

ARE ALIENS REALLY REAL?

Are aliens really real?
Why do they have long eyes,
On those little, thin tubes
And how do they move?

Are aliens really real?
Why are they so tall and skinny
With tall legs and arms
And those fingers which are big?

Are aliens really real?
Why are they all different colours
Green, red, yellow, blue
With really weird-shaped heads?

Are aliens really real?

Adam Brewster (12)
Cromwell Community College

MY BEST EXCUSE YET

My alien is blue, Miss,
Yes blue!
Well, not totally blue
He's blue with green spots
He has ten eyes, Miss,
And he eats a lot.
My homework got in the hands
And well . . .
He ate it, then spat it out
It's true Miss, it is . . .!

Harrison Salter (11)
Cromwell Community College

Ruin, Sorrow and Death

As the cards are turned over
My future is revealed,
My friends before me
Were promised a fair deal
Ruin, sorrow and death
Are upon mine,
I must be careful
The cards never lie.

My future is deep,
Dark and dreary,
I'm screaming so loud
Can no one hear me?
All my dreams and ambitions
Lost down the drain,
Just like the street dirt
Washed away by the rain
I believed that my life
Was forever divine
This can't be the truth
If the cards never lie.

Bryel Parnell (14)
Cromwell Community College

No More Excuses

It was an alien that came from the sky,
That took my pen and tried to fly,
They dropped it on the Milky Way,
The ship ran over it in half a day,
That's the reason why, sir,
It's not a lie!

Dawn Gleaves (11)
Cromwell Community College

MY THREE FAVOURITE STAR SIGNS

People born as Scorpio
Always think they ought to know
Never say that they are wrong
They might find out, it won't take long.

People born as Gemini
Never really want to try
It's alright saying let's do this,
It won't get done.

People born as Capricorn
Always sleep and never yawn
It's funny how I realise
When I yawn it feels real nice

In case you wonder I'm Scorpio
Do you believe this? I don't know.

Julie Heading (12)
Cromwell Community College

ALIENS

Huge, fuzzy eyes the size of eggs,
Huge, funny heads the shape of footballs
With long, skinny, green legs.
I wonder how their aircraft fly.
Tall, skinny bodies
Do they have thunder?
Do they throw paddies?

I wonder?

Thomas Salisbury (12)
Cromwell Community College

SCHOOL DAYS

Teachers teach,
Children screech,
Long narrow corridors
Lots of different classroom doors
Then tall children swarming
Move out the way (warning).
Bells ringing,
Ears singing,
Chalk scrapping away at the pitch-black board (fast)
Today's nearly over at last
I shall never forget this first day
Not for a while anyway.

Freya Robinson (11)
Cromwell Community College

ALIENS

I saw an alien from Mars,
He bought me a vase.

I saw an alien on the sun,
He was fun.

I saw an alien in the classroom,
That was my teacher!

I saw an alien on the moon,
He took me home too soon!

I saw an alien,
Just like you!

Keeley Hardman (11)
Cromwell Community College

BIG SISTERS

Sisters smell,
They don't behave well,
They think they're cool,
They're very, very dull.
They make a mess,
They're a big pest.
They stuff their face,
They're a big disgrace,
They chat on the phone,
They really do moan,
They chat up the boys,
They nick all the toys,
They read boring books,
All they think about is their looks,
They're sisters!

Michelle Smalley (11)
Cromwell Community College

MARS

The red planet
    Burning, like a flame
Hot as molten rock
    Lava in orbit.

Lying in wait for exploration
    Fourth from the sun
A neighbour to Earth for light years
    The bringer of war is burning.

Charlotte Roberts (11)
Cromwell Community College

My Magic Poem

G etting on with each other
O nly once a week
O pening doors with a creak
D own the school path we go.

F inding new friends
R eason for not handing it in
I go to school
E very day
N aughty children getting into trouble
D ance is on at lunch times
S chool is over now, we can go home.

Laura Allen (11)
Cromwell Community College

Sports Days

S wimming is my favourite sport
P laying different kinds of sport
O n sports day we run
R unning keeps you fit
T oday there is a football match
S ometimes we play hockey.

D ecember is the month for ice skating
A lways do your best in sport
Y esterday we played cricket
S oon we will have games - hooray!

Stephen Reed (11)
Cromwell Community College

THE BEAUTY OF SPACE

Z igzagging stars fly across the sky
O ctarine lights brighten the night
D own on Earth, the view is great
I magine being in the middle of space
A round the sun and back again
C onstellations give us light and fun.

Victoria Weatherby (13)
Cromwell Community College

PLUTO'S ALIENS

P luto's
L arge
A liens live on
N eptune, who blew up
E arth which was
T erribly
S ad.

Lloyd White (12)
Cromwell Community College

SILENT STARS

S ilence is the sound
T he shining stars
A re so bright
R ivers of little light
S himmering sight.

Helen Pitkin (13)
Cromwell Community College

FUTURE FANTASY

A car in the sky,
Pigs will fly,
But I don't think so!
But so they say
What will the future hold?
Nothing,
Or
Everything,
The world will explode,
Get abducted by aliens
And go to other planets on holiday?
Who knows what the future will hold?
Let's wait and see . . .

Steven Reid (14)
Cromwell Community College

MIAMI

Guns, guns,
Bang, bang,
Kill, kill,
Call 911, 911,
Fighting with guns
Someone dead,
Hooligan running with his gang,
Gun thrown away,
They hide,
Noise comes towards them.
The next day the gang is normal.
Think!

Karl Tanner (14)
Cromwell Community College

WILL IT TASTE NICE?

Is this right?
Taking a big, fat bite?
Will it taste nice?
Is it as hard as raw rice?

Will I spit it out?
Will I scream and shout?
Am I going to be sick?
Am I that thick?

Maybe I might be?
But do people see the real me?
What am I waiting for?
I don't think anyone saw?

Yyyyuuuuuummmmm!

Grace Housley-Stott (11)
Cromwell Community College

WHAT WILL BE THE FUTURE?

What will be the future,
When we are gone and dead?
The generations yet to come
They only move ahead.
They never give a single thought,
Of people from the past.
We're the ones who fought the wars,
To keep them moving fast
Walk towards the future,
But don't forget about the past.

Samantha Rex (14)
Cromwell Community College

DESTINY

Staring at the sky at night
Gazing at the stars
I think of all the years before,
How in my mind they've lasted.

I wonder if my life's been set,
Every trip or fall,
And every road I've wandered down,
Is at the stars beck and call.

My life lies out before me,
Has my future been foretold?
Every day a mystery,
A secret each one holds.

Maybe the stars choose my fate,
Or maybe it's my own wit,
There's only one thing I believe,
That life's what *you* make of it!

Kathlene Cavilla (14)
Cromwell Community College

BROTHERS AND SISTERS

Brothers are pains,
They steal everything.
Sisters are annoying,
If they're younger than you.
Brothers always fight with you,
Sisters block up the bath.
Trust me you don't want a brother,
Nor do you want a sister!

Natalie Rayner (11)
Cromwell Community College

I Don't Know

Is there a man in the moon?
Are the stars balls of fire?
Is the sun a hot lava?
I don't know!

Is the moon made of cheese?
Are the twinkling stars little fairies?
Is the sun a massive ball of fire?
I don't know!

Has the moon got holes in which worms come out?
Do the stars have five points?
Is the sun a really hot planet?
I don't know!

Is the moon a cold planet?
Are the stars comets?
Does the sun have rays sticking out at all angles?
I don't know.

Kirsty Farrington (12)
Cromwell Community College

Spiders

There are cobwebs in my room
There are cobwebs in my room,
We'll get them very soon,
We'll get them with a broom.
Creepy-crawly spiders
Climbing up their webs,
Scream, then squash them dead!

Lisa Nicholas (13)
Cromwell Community College

HOROSCOPE

Monday, the twenty-seventh of May
For you a very exciting day.
At home you'll receive some well-earned praise,
From a loved one who's
Going through a moody phase.
At work money isn't flowing fast,
Be careful, your job may no longer last
In the world of love
Things are going well
Destiny sees a name beginning with L.
At a party tonight, be careful what you say
You may offend someone in a terrible way.
Luck stares at an old wine tumbler
For more information please call this number:
000 22 00000 1.

Jonathan Clarke (14)
Cromwell Community College

ANIMAL SOUNDS

Cats miaowing,
Dogs howling,
Snakes hissing,
Otters swimming.

Gophers hiding,
Parrots talking,
Sharks feeding,
Crabs pinching.

Matthew Smith (13)
Cromwell Community College

NED!

I once had a friend called Ned
Who always believed what he read
He woke every morning
But before he was yawning
He picked up the paper instead.
He flicked passed the news,
The cinema reviews
To the back of the paper which said . . .

His star sign a Libra he always believed her,
No matter what the old girl had said
His death overdue, he'd have to pursue
Just cuts and bruises instead!

Lewis Aitcheson (14)
Cromwell Community College

IN THE MUSIC ROOM

Ping, pang the xylophones rang
'For we ring . . .' the children would sing
Tap, bang, tap the drum set would rap
'Get out!' the teacher would shout.
Toot, toot, toot the recorder would hoot
The CD is in, instruments in the bin.
Dum, dee, dum the guitar would strum
Screech, screech, toot went the flute
Tap, ring, tap the tambourine rapped
The record player played, new music was made
Bang! Boom! Bang! Boom!
A typical day in the music room.

Amy Lince (12)
Cromwell Community College

DEATH IN THE SKY

Glittering stars attacked the sky,
As the angry clouds drifted by.
The silent moon was hidden away,
As if it were a summer day.

The velvet sky was the darkest black,
While the moon beams stabbed it in the back.
The shooting stars were living bombs,
While planets in the darkness sing lonely songs.

A vicious storm is brewing in the night,
Then the lightning strikes in a ball of blinding light.
Ripping apart the deathly sky,
With the whimpering thunder's dying cry.

The blood rain falls down at the end of the night,
Then everything stops, it's the end of the fight.

Zoe Peverill (14)
Cromwell Community College

PLANETS

P lanets are the shape of a sphere
L ight comes from the sun which is a planet
A nd light comes from the moon
N ever look directly at the sun
E arth is the third planet in the solar system
T ime stands still in space
S aturn is a planet with a ring around its body.

Laura Edgley (12)
Cromwell Community College

BLIND DATE HOROSCOPE

I didn't want to read it,
I didn't want to dare,
So I'm waiting for my blind date
Pretending not to care.

Maybe it is this one,
He's handsome and well fit,
I love his bulging biceps,
He reminds me of Brad Pitt.

Or maybe it is this one,
He's tall and rather thin,
He's munching from a burger box,
He just got from the bin.

Oh surely it's not this one,
Who's selling the Big Issue,
But looking at his snotty nose,
I think he needs a tissue.

And still I'm standing waiting,
And getting very wet,
I've given up my chance of love,
My blind date I've not met.

I know I shouldn't have read it
I knew I shouldn't have cared,
I wish I'd turned the other cheek,
From torture I'd been spared.

Hollie Wootton (14)
Cromwell Community College

THE MISSING STAR SIGN

I looked up to the stars in January,
And saw the stars of Capricorn.
I looked up to the stars in February,
I saw the stars of Aquarius.
I looked up to the stars in March,
And saw the stars of Pisces.
I looked up to the stars in April,
I saw the stars of Aries.
I looked up to the stars in May,
And saw the stars of Taurus.
I looked up to the stars in June,
I saw the stars of Gemini.
I looked up to the stars in July,
And saw the stars of Cancer.
I looked up to the stars in August,
I saw the stars of Leo,
I looked up to the stars in September,
And saw the stars of Virgo.
I looked up to the stars in October,
I saw the stars of Libra.
I looked up to the stars in November,
And saw the stars of Scorpio.
I looked up to the stars in December,
But where was the last of them all?

Emma Watkins (14)
Cromwell Community College

LOVE AND MEN

Love and men just do not mix.
They think it's a load of mumbo-jumbo.
They think they can win us over
With a bunch of flowers and a Twix.
Well, as you know, they can't.

Love and men just do not mix.
They surround you with a sloppy, old kiss.
But then again when the football's on they sit on their bums and say
'Darling, can you make us a cup of tea?'

Love and men.

Sarah Jane Snow (11)
Cromwell Community College

A MAP OF THE STARS

Venus, Earth, Uranus, and Mars
Each burning brightly, each a star.
Virgo the princess of long lasting love
Cancer, Scorpio, Leo all shimmering above.
Deep in the blackness known as universe
Two star signs crossing is known as a curse.
The planets and stars all form different signs
Wacky, weird patterns or simple, straight lines.
Geminis stand untied as twins
Libra as scales gently swing
Pisces swim together in the sky
All this time the atmosphere spins by -
The Taurus bull charges straight at Saturn
Right through the plough disturbing its pattern
Well that's just about all from our zodiac friends
Did I mention Capricorn, the list never ends.
Tarot cards reveal your destiny
A fortune teller can foresee
Is it a good thing we may ask,
A perfect stranger revealing our past?
For some it's an addiction
To reveal their prediction
While others couldn't care less!

Zoe Feast (14)
Cromwell Community College

MY RECORD BARBEL

Down on the River Avon,
Barbel were my target,
I set up the hoards of tackle,
In this perfect haven.
I cast out the baits, into the raging water,
Then down from the forest came my grandparents' daughter,
I got one twitch on my rod tip,
Then a squirrel jumped from tree to tree with an impressive flip
My mum went back up through the woods with my insane dog Zack,
I got a take on my right-hand rod
And the line went crack
I felt very sad down inside and cast the rod back out,
Ten minutes later I got a bite and gave my dad a shout.
Then after a spirited fight I got it to the net,
I then lifted it onto the bank where it got me soaking wet.
We lifted it up onto the scales,
It weighed in at sixteen pounds four,
I had twenty-five photos taken,
Now I wanted more.
The next night we had a barbecue and a bottle of champagne,
To celebrate my extraordinary catch,
I had started another record reign.
The night after we went down to the river,
Then put out all the rods,
As I sat upon my chair I got a take on my quiver,
I was into another barbel,
This one was not quite as big,
But at fourteen pounds five ounce
It finished off my holiday with records to announce.

Ryan Gibson (14)
Cromwell Community College

MY THOUGHTS ON STAR SIGNS

The symbol of Sagittarius is weird but wonderful,
It's powerful and its presence is felt,
Its hind legs are strong and overpowering,
It has the lower body of a horse and the upper body of a human,
It holds a bow and arrow in its gripping hands,
It looks like it is an unbeatable giant.

The symbol of Libra is amazing and law abiding,
The scale swings side to side with the thoughts of temptation
                                                    and good will,
It stands with its arms out wide,
Breaching into the great, wide world,
It looks powerful and enforcing,
It is quick to judge, but forgiving.

The symbol of Aries is proud and commanding
It stands on its muscular hind legs,
It has horrifying horns on the top of its cautious cranium,
Its coat is woolly yet firm,
There is also a whole different world in its eyes,
A scary but amazing world.

John Cole (14)
Cromwell Community College

THE ELEPHANT

There once was an elephant called Fred,
He did once have a mother, but now she was dead!
He took monkeys for rides,
And fell down mud slides,
That silly elephant, Fred!

Sophie English (11)
Cromwell Community College

SEA DEPTHS

The sea depths are so dark
Like a horror park.
There are underwater lakes of silt
An eel is nearby, it leaves its prey, as if it has guilt.
There are horrors awaiting you
Mouths agape to swallow you
The sea depths are like this,
You know that blue abyss
Through this all
There is a ghostly call
Past the anglerfish like stars
Its eyes as red as Mars,
Swims a creature,
The sea's main feature,
It swims higher
Like a climber
It jumps up high
Emits a cry
It goes back to what it left
In the sea depths.

Lucy White (12)
Cromwell Community College

SPIDER

There's a spider in my room
I'm going to swipe it with my broom
Please can someone get it out of here?
There is a spider in my room
I can't go upstairs to go to sleep
Because there's a spider in my room!

Craig Barnes (13)
Cromwell Community College

WITCHES SPELL

The witches gathered in a circle
Under the stars so bright
Chanting verses,
Reciting spells,
With only candles for their light.
The five each stood at a corner
Of the pentacle in the sand
Their heads all bowed
Their hands all joined
Chanting ancient words
When silence fell upon them
And they stood as still as rocks
Each candle died
One by one
A corner at a time
Then ten miles away
Under the glow of the full moon
A body rose up from the ground
And stood
Still
Waiting for its next command.

Tanith Hayward (15)
Cromwell Community College

HORSES

Horses are like planets
Warm-blooded like Mercury,
Cold-blooded like Pluto,
Angry like Mars or
Gentle like Venus.

Vicky Bannister (12)
Cromwell Community College

DIDN'T YOU KNOW?

Some are described by animals,
And some everyday objects,
They're in newspapers and in magazines,
And on the radio,
I think you know what I'm talking about,
I think you just might know.

Signs of the zodiac!

Virgo is a lady,
Dressed from head to toe in white.
Leo is a lion,
That only comes out at night.

Cancer is the red crab,
That clips, clips, clips.
Capricorn is the goat,
That kicks, kicks, kicks.

Pisces is the fish,
That bubbles all the time.
Gemini are twins,
That talk, talk, talk and talk!

Scorpio's the scorpion,
Extremely powerful and aggressive.
Aries is the dreadful ram,
Strong, determined, forceful, born leaders.

Taurus is the bull,
Strong like Aries.
Libra is the scales,
They're well balanced.

> Which leaves me with Aquarius,
> A lighter version of Scorpio.
> Don't forget Sagittarius,
> That's my star sign didn't you know?

Stephanie Boyden (12)
Cromwell Community College

I'M THE PAST AND FUTURE

My past was dreadful,
People laughing at me
I feel so ugly,
Cannot breath,
Since I'm suffering from depression,
I hate myself,
Myself and my dreadful childhood.

I can change,
I can change,
I can learn from my mistakes.

My future will be fine,
People will know that I'm human,
I feel so proud,
I can talk,
Since I know how to communicate,
I like myself,
Myself and my brilliant future.

I have changed,
I have changed,
I'm more human,
I'm more human,
I'm a human!

John Gleaves (14)
Cromwell Community College

PLANETS

P lanets are in space,
L ying in a bed of stars,
A liens live up
N ights go by
E ver wondered what's up there?
T he man on the moon or
S atellites in the sky?

Kelly Burrows (12)
Cromwell Community College

SPIDER

There's a spider in my room
I'm gonna get it with my broom
So, spider in my room
Watch out for that broom!

Matthew Lacey (13)
Cromwell Community College

JAKE - HISSELF

My name is Jake,
My favourite colour's blue,
I drink Dr Pepper,
My favourite car is BMW,
I like rock music,
How about you?

Marcus Clarke (11)
Manor Community College

KATIE IS...

She's a beautiful, blue summer's sky,
And fizzy Fanta, fizzing in your eye.

She's as funky as a probe with flashing lights,
As calm as autumn and peaceful nights.

She's as spicy as curry with rice,
As cuddly as a penguin on the ice.

She's a squashy as a sofa to sit on or lay,
And wild as reggae to dance to all day.

She's as groovy as three quarter lengths in a draw,
And as sparkly as a gem worth a million and more!

Natalie Edwards (12)
Manor Community College

CATS

Light shining brightly in a cat's face,
Makes its eyes glow,
Its fur long, smooth and soft,
The colour of snow.

The cat's waiting, waiting to play,
Just sitting there patiently to catch its prey,
The way its tail waggles in the air,
Is like a worm slithering on the ground,
The way it miaows is like a piercing lion sound.

Felicity Price (11)
Manor Community College

A Poem About David Beckham

He's a bright, fiery red,
He's a pint of extra strong Red Bull,
He's a speedy sports car
And a summer's day.
He's a packet of high energy sweets,
He's a fierce tiger,
He's a big, black chair,
He's rap music,
He's a red Man Utd shirt.

Michael Kember (11)
Manor Community College

For My Poor Dead Mum

Your smile reminds me of a warm, sunny yellow
And a lovely bottle of wine.
You make me think of a peaceful Mini
On a wet summer's day climb.
You loved to make Sunday roast
And you've been the best mum really.
You always loved to take a nap
But a graceful swan is you truly . . .

Emily Hall (11)
Manor Community College

My Mum

She's a bright, blue sky
With as shot of Southern Comfort,
Speeding down a mountain road in a Voyager,
Sitting out on a hot summer's day,
Eating a twenty ounce steak,

Walking her Staffordshire bull terrier,
Jumping on her leather sofa,
Listening to pop music,
Wearing sport clothes,
While wearing her necklace.

Jamie Thomas (12)
Manor Community College

SHE IS . . .

She's dark blue like night-time sea
And a warm cup of tea.
She's a bright green jeep wondering through the desert
And she's a cold winter's day.
She's a cheese burger with chips on the side,
And she's like a big, strong horse.
She is a big armchair which she likes to sleep in.
She's a wonderful pop star with a brilliant voice
And a pair of old jeans that never wear out.
She shines like her wishbone ring.

Sarah Watson (11)
Manor Community College

ALL ABOUT MARCUS AND HIS FAVOURITE THINGS

He's a clear ocean blue,
He's a tall bubbling Sprite,
He's a flash, red and shiny Ferrari,
He's a hot summer's day,
He's a chocolate fudge cake mixed with custard,
He's a green alien,
He's Marcus!

Jake Rowland (11)
Manor Community College

My Little Brother

He is a bright and beautiful, billowing blue,
He's a rouge Ribena swirling round in a glass,
A mini limousine scooting round mountain peeks,
He is creme puffs and chocolate muffins melting in your mouth,
He's hip hop music, boppin' everywhere,
                    singing 'Who Let The Dogs Out?'
Little baby booties represent him strolling to the park,
And a fluffy shag pile rug, tickling your toes,
He is a cuddly, soft and warm baby bear playing with A, B, C, blocks
                    by the fire,
He's a twinkling diamond shining bright like the ones in his eyes,
But best of all, he's my little brother.

Rochelle Ebanks (11)
Manor Community College

My Mum

When I am naughty my mum is a vicious red,
When I am in bed my mum is as cool as wine.
She is a Ferrari going down the motorway really fast,
She is a nice, hot summer's day,
My mum is a nice, calm shark swimming in the sea,
My mum is a nice, hot dish of bolognese,
My mum is a comfortable leather sofa,
She is a nice bit of music,
She is a nice, warm jumper,
She is as cuddly as a teddy,
She is as precious as a diamond to me.

Kieran Delph (11)
Manor Community College

NATALIE IS . . .

She's a sunset orange looking over the sea,
A glass of fizzy lemonade, as fizzy as can be.
She is my dream, silver BMW speeding down the road
And a beautiful spring afternoon as the birds sing in their own code.
She's warm, tasty fish fingers steaming on a plate,
A baby Tigger playing with her best mate,
She's a nice squashy bed, bouncing 24/7,
She's relaxing classical music, playing as I fall to sleep,
                              in a dream of heaven,
She's a glittery non-sleeve top as it catches everyone's eye,
And she's the shiniest diamond in the world, as it glances at the
                                                people walking by.

Katie Asby (11)
Manor Community College

SHE IS . . .

She's a gentle pink like fresh blossom falling from a new tree,
A steaming cup of tea, with biscuits to dunk.
She's a speeding Mercedes along forest roads during the winter months.

She's like warm hot dogs with chips on the side,
A small, fluffy rabbit with a small bob tail running through the fields,
She's pop music and a comfy sofa to fall asleep on,
She's a long, purple skirt embroidered with silk
                              along with a special signet ring.

Hannah Mallows (11)
Manor Community College

AN AUTUMN HEART

The leaves are falling
And turning brown.
You can't hear a word,
A whistle, a sound.

The dew has come,
The web is shown.
How much I wish
I was at home.

The darkness is falling,
The night has come.
I feel my fingers and toes
Go numb.

The wheat is growing
In the fields.
It will soon be ready
For the harvest meal.

I'm walking home,
Back through the park,
And now I have an
Autumn heart!

Jenny Crawford (11)
Orton Longueville School

A Tunnel To Freedom

Dumped in a tunnel
There's no route back
There is a light
But can I reach it?

I proceed slowly
On my trip
The darkness is deathly to me
As is the loneliness.

Traps, randomly dispersed attempt to pull me down
Their weight burdens me
At first they were featherweight
But now there are too many.

My life is so much slower
As if someone has dammed the flow of time.

The light is close now
I can see the end
Freedom
It's not for me
I am too heavy,
My strength finally has left me
To the darkness . . .

Robin Smid (11)
Oundle & Laxton Schools

AGA SAGA

My family collect around me,
Undeterred by my iron clad exterior;
They have discovered the warmth within,
And I protect them.

Little do they remember that day,
When a frost-bitten clammy creature,
Clothed in mud, was entrusted to me.
I revived her.

I know I am appreciated;
Visitors to my home are jealous,
But I dread the summer,
Those long, insufferable days . . .

They leave me switched on.
When my previously welcome heat becomes a burden,
Even the family cat deserts me in my hour of need.

Some time ago,
A little into the coldest month of the year,
I went on strike.

But the punishments inflicted!
Such torture -
Spiny little implements inserted into me,
Twisted and turned in an attempt to end my act of rebellion.

That one week of vengeance
I regretted for the rest of my life . . .
A usurper arrived.

This puny inferior attempted to steal my role as Kitchen Queen,
Horrified, I re-ignited at once;
But it was too late.
Our relationship could never be the same,
With Microwave beside me.

But I am old now
And I know that one day
I shall be replaced.
I consider the times I held my family's comfort in my furnace . . .
And wonder at mankind's inconstancy.

Kate Mason (13)
Oundle & Laxton Schools

SHE STILL BELIEVED THAT PEOPLE WERE REALLY GOOD AT HEART

For the two terrifying years,
Cooped up in an attic,
Wondering what was going on outside,
Wondering what was going to happen,
She sat writing her diary,
Watching and waiting.

As a baby bird,
Seeking freedom from her nest.

But then there was a knock,
A shooting of guns,
A piercing scream from below,
She stood frozen to the spot.
They had found us.

Freedom,
Freedom,
She was grateful to be captured,
Grateful for the sunshine and fresh air.

But then, all was quiet,
She was gone.

Katherine Bullard (11)
Oundle & Laxton Schools

AN UNFOLDING STORY

Anne Frank,
Her life,
A story unfolding.
She runs an obstacle course
But doesn't quite reach the end.
She climbs a tall brick wall,
Not quite at the top
She falls.
Falls down to the ground.
Being brave she picks herself up,
Picks herself up and tries again.

The fear and terror she encounters,
Is like a never-ending staircase
Winding and winding upwards,
Stairs that are hard to climb
Fear that is hard to overcome
She climbs forever
Until she is rescued.
Rescued from death,
A glimmer of hope shining,
A light she only dreamed of.

Finally free, she walks the land
Rummaging for food in dustbins,
Like a lion searching for prey
She finds nothing.
The fear of death she once escaped
Has come back to haunt her.

Amy Shaw (11)
Oundle & Laxton Schools

Your Pathway To Death

I am a snake,
My poisonous fangs shimmer in the light,
I bite any victim,
Kill any organism,
I am your pathway to death.

She is my prey,
Her reassuring laugh and soft smile,
Her dark hair and strange eyes,
Her faith, her religion,
Her existence.

She is a mouse in the forest,
Scuttling around on all fours,
Trying to hide under logs or in holes,
She will never conceal herself from me,
I am her pathway to death.

She hid from me once,
I unveiled her camouflage,
I made her suffer,
I punished her forever stepping onto this planet,
And now she is deceased.

I am not ashamed of what I did,
I probably never will be,
I am not a soft animal you can stroke,
I am fierce and feared by all,
I am their pathway to death.

Hannah Matthews (11)
Oundle & Laxton Schools

THE WAY TO DIE

The way to die is the way I want,
To have the eternal sleep,
To be buried in my coffin,
Where my new life begins.

Although everyone says death is bad,
I feel happy to have reached the gate.
To be reunited with my family
To be remembered by those I knew.

This place might be just as good,
To have fun, to sing and play
Like a cat with a mouse
To have freedom next to me.

Here seems better because no one will harm us,
There are no food rations so we can eat,
On earth I grew weak because of small food,
But oh no not here.

I'm not sure if this is Heaven
But it feels like it!

Khadija Kachra (11)
Oundle & Laxton Schools

RUN AND SHOUT

I'm being locked away in this attic,
Like a prisoner in his cell,
Just this is only worse.

I've made only one friend since I've been here
The rest, I am at war,
The one I had disliked is now my only friend.

I wish so much to be outside,
Where I can run and shout in rays,
But all day we sit, miserable and wait.

When the sitting is over,
Only vicious fights will start,
I always make it worse by opening my mouth.

Grass and sunshine are right next door,
But a wall boldly in the way,
The door is waiting for me, when the green police have gone.

Anything would be better than this,
Even those labouring death camps,
At least I'm outside doing . . .

Huw Dawson (11)
Oundle & Laxton Schools

DEAR DIARY

How I long to walk outside
In the meadows, woods and streets.
To shout, laugh, run and be free,
Is all a child could want.

I often look out of the window
And see the children play.
How I wish I could be there,
Rather than in here.

While I creep and tiptoe around
Until the workmen go.
I learn all my school lessons
From Father during the day.
With only Peter to play with,
I often feel alone.

I sometimes dream of the green police
Breaking in to get us.
We're all afraid, we'll soon be found,
Like the rest of them.

Amila Subramaniam (11)
Oundle & Laxton Schools

DEAR GOD

Dear God, can you hear me up there?
I want to tell you a story,
The story of my life then and now,
The story of the attic.

The attic is
Dark, bare of sunlight
A world of gloom,
Of silence.

Never
I will not resign myself,
I will not surrender.
Out there a war is raging,
In here there is one too.

A battle between dark and light,
But really it's a battle within myself,
Never will I give up to the fact that niggles at my mind
The fact that this is my life.

Why, oh why, God,
Was I born at
This time,
This place,
To this family?

War

My heart bubbles with hatred,
A volcano about to erupt,
A cauldron soon to over boil,
No.

I mustn't think these things,
Or I'll be giving myself up
To bitterness,
Like a contrary old man.

Because,
'In spite of everything I still believe that people are really good at heart.'

I hope I am too, God.

Amen.

Shanna Martens (11)
Oundle & Laxton Schools

SOUR, BITTER OR SWEET

Which one are you?

The tongue . . .

You can't hide from it:
It will find you out,
It will seek out your intimate flavour.
Break through your shell,
Get to the true taste inside.

It might be rash at first:
Dislike you because of your reputation.
But when it gets used to you.
It will think you're the
Sweetest thing since treacle.

It may have a grudge against you though,
And if so there's nothing you can do.

Sour, bitter or sweet
Which one are you?

Harriet Scriven (11)
Oundle & Laxton Schools

WHO LIT THE FIRE? WE'LL NEVER KNOW

A small layer on top of the tree
That we all depend upon,
Here I live, discreetly, alone,
Looking at the world,
Yet it does not recognise my presence.

I eat away at my home
As time goes on,
Taking only what I can afford to.

The many rings are like the layers
That keep me chained away
We live in fear
Of being chopped down with our home
Or found by curious, unwanted creatures,
We cannot escape it, night or day.

We have had close encounters before
But this time was different
We heard the crackling
It was like a warning siren,
Yet where could we run to?
We could do nothing but stand there, petrified ad wait,
The smoke drove us out,
Then the flames consumed us,
Who lit the fire? We'll never know.

Alice McDonald (11)
Oundle & Laxton Schools

I WISH . . .

I shall die soon,
Ridden with pity and sorrow,
Ready for death, like a lost ship,
Wasting away on the bottom of the sea.

I wish to eliminate heartlessness,
Poverty and hate,
I shall wish even through death.

I wish for Peter to live,
As I love him dearly, he is pure to the heart
He made my life liveable as we struggled on.

I give my heart to Mouschi as he,
Was Peter's soul possession
Like a small fragment he would be lost without.

I am attached to life like a spider has bound me to the web of life
I am just one of many people
Trying to escape its grasp.

My last wish, please preserve the outside air
As that is my first love,
Like a second area of my life.

Rosalie Brooman-White (11)
Oundle & Laxton Schools

MY FAVOURITE FLOWER

People there are many, but friends there are few
When I feel trapped or unsure what to do
There's you.

You are there when I need help
Or when I feel like I don't want to live
You give.

When you give me your time
Your thoughts and advice,
Your love.

Love from an angel like you are
Makes me think how lucky I am you were sent
From above.

As a flower needs the sun
To grow and to live
I need you.

Forever,
For eternity,
For you, my favourite flower.

Victoria Bonnici (15)
St Bede's School, Cambridge

MY CAT JESS

I have a loveable cat called Jess
Who always gets the house in a mess
She eats Whiskas Complete
Which helps keep her on her feet
She's soft, cuddly and pure white
And *boy*, can she see in the night!

Jessica Marsh (11)
St Bede's School, Cambridge

THE STORM

Silence,
A breeze through the trees,
Shaking the leaves.
Rustling,
The cold winter wind,
Cuts through you like a blade,
And sends shivers down your back,
Like an earthquake.

Shifting and shuffling,
Clouds blow over,
And turn the sky as dark as night.
Wind turns to gale,
And lifts objects with ease,
Tossing them round and round,
Like a washing machine.

Mother Nature's tears are icy cold,
Falling harder and harder,
Splash! They reach their end on the watery ground.
Flash! Streaks of light as white as the moon,
Cut the night sky in half,
Trees are torn up and snapped,
Like matchsticks,
And scattered about the chaotic land.

Wind and water disappear
Clouds disperse,
The sun appears from its hiding place,
Silence.

Nick Lamble (13)
St Bede's School, Cambridge

AUTUMN MORNING

The morning breaks to a hazy mist
The sun hides somewhere in the sky
A cobweb carpet covers the garden,
Another day is dawning.

A gentle breeze begins to lift the mist
The sun's rays break through the clouds
The garden turns green as the cobwebs dissolve
Another day is forming.

Alarm goes off at seven, I wake then get ready for school
Eat my breakfast in a hurry, pack my bags, brush my hair
Mother's shouting 'You'll be late'
I take note of my mother's warning.

Walking to the bus stop,
Kicking leaves, fallen from the trees
Dry, crisp, brown and noisy
Another autumn morning.

Deborah Few (11)
St Bede's School, Cambridge

JODIE'S ELEPHANT

Jodie went to the zoo one day, Jodie went to the zoo.
She saw the elephants having a bath and then she named one Lou.
He wet his head, he filled his trunk, he blew it up in the air.
Jodie got wet, her mummy got wet, the water was everywhere.

'I like it here at the zoo, especially my elephant Lou,
He may have wet me,
He may have soaked me,
But I still like my elephant Lou.'

Zoe Cox (11)
St Bede's School, Cambridge

THE GYPSY

As I walked into the dark, gloomy room,
I saw her staring into space,
Like a director had commanded pause on her life,
She sat there, empty.

I wasn't sure whether she had seen me,
Because she turned and stared,
But I had a terrible boding,
That she could look into my soul.

'Cross my palm with silver,'
She slyly croaked,
And she held out her wizened hand,
For her bounty.

As she raised the cloth from her crystal ball,
The mists cleared,
Suddenly my future was unmistakable,
Fate would decide.

Stacey Purath (14)
St Bede's School, Cambridge

WAR

The man's blood was like a river,
Flowing down a mountain.
The screams and shouts
Where all about
And I thought, Mum can I come home now
But I stayed because I was brave
Fighting for my country.

Jamie Simms (11)
St Bede's School, Cambridge

WHAT HAS THE WORLD COME TO?

In the dark alleyway a cat purrs,
Looking in through a window, a child cries,
Look around the corner, a man held at gun point,
Laying in the road, a successful murder.

What has the world come to?
What? I ask,
That cold murder can be performed with no trace.

Screams echo the dark, midnight sky,
A car alarm shrills through a once quiet street,
Drunk men steer themselves into the illuminated clubs,
Gallons of alcohol wasted for fun.

What has the world come to?
What? I ask,
Respectful it was, but now,
No class.

Karl Walker (14)
St Bede's School, Cambridge

FOLLOWING YOU

Cutting the puppet strings
To our souls
Destroying the spineless
Who rule our world
To dream a dream
No one else has seen
To dare to be
Beaten to dust

And survive.

Jemima Estabrook (15)
St Bede's School, Cambridge

OUR FUTURE

What will there be in the future?
A question so many of us ask.
Will there be peace
Between all the nations?
Or violent wars
Filled with complications?
I often ask myself,
If I will see
A world full of love,
And all countries in unity.
But then I stop,
I think of my life.
I should think of *now*,
Not future troubles and strife.
I needn't even think of tomorrow!

Hannah Megson (13)
St Bede's School, Cambridge

WAR

The explosions; the gunshots are common sounds,
The blood-red sky of a new morning of fighting!
Sadly soldiers wander to their trenches,
Suddenly a terrific noise like a giant crash of thunder,
Then the tragedy comes, seven dead,
Innocent people serving their country,
Not their fault! No one's fault!
War, a terrible thing, the fear of most!
Who wins? No one!
The joy of no one.

Jack Scotney (11)
St Bede's School, Cambridge

THE CAT

The cat wriggled through a hole in the brown brick wall
And jumped up onto an apple tree.

The cat then looked down upon the great, green grass,
And noticed a blue bird pecking at some crusty bread.

The cat leapt and sped away after the pecking bird
The bird looked up and gazed, lazily at the cat
And with one final look the bird flew away.

The cat groaned with disappointment
And crawled under an emerald bush
To wait for its next prey.

The cat's eyes began to droop . . .

Rachel Moden (13)
St Bede's School, Cambridge

WINTER

As snowflakes start to fall
Icicles start to form
Decent sledges come out to play
Terrible frost sticking everywhere like jam on toast
Excited, raging children come out to muck around
They start to make massive snowballs as big as footballs
The time whizzes past like a dog chasing a cat
All the children go inside
Yet waiting for another cold day
Sleepy time for all children.

Danielle Ball (12)
St Bede's School, Cambridge

ABYSS

The shadows bloom
In the dark crevice of night
The howlings of the malevolent wind
Echo for eternity
There is a blackness, deadlier than death himself
A path worse than fate.
There is a bitter sorcery
An unseen magic
Never to be uttered.
A venomous veil has been drawn,
A way will be chosen
A choice made
A soul swallowed
Plunged into the depths of oblivion.

Anna Hornby (13)
St Bede's School, Cambridge

THE WEATHER

Oh I hate the rain
Cold, wet and muddy.
Oh I hate the sun
Hot, sweaty and sunny.
Coats, gloves and hats
Shorts, glasses and caps.
Umbrellas, can't go out to play
Ice lollies, can't stand the heat.
Oh I wish it was snowing
Sledging, snowmen, having fun
Oh I wish it was snowing.

Suzanne Patterson (12)
St Bede's School, Cambridge

ASHES TO ASHES

Ashes to ashes,
Dust to dust,
The drugs I took were a powdered dust.
I became edgy alert,
The others revert.
My sight blurred,
Nerves slowed.
Justice was perverted,
Parents' eyes averted.
I was stunned,
My body numbed,
Ashes to ashes,
Dust to dust,
I just died, sniffing that magical dust.
RIP.

Scott Collen (13)
St Bede's School, Cambridge

WHY?

September 11th 2001.

Life so precious
What gives you the right
To seize it, steal it, snatch the years away?
Terrorist of mind, insane
You don't kill hope
You *will* feel pain
America will rise again,
A phoenix from the ashes.

Claire Hancock (14)
St Bede's School, Cambridge

WEATHER

The weather changes with different seasons,
Because of many different reasons.
From storm to thunder, sun to rain,
Ice, snow and hurricanes
It's windy and rainy, wet and dry,
As clouds race across the sky.
The wind makes the trees dance and sway
Throwing their leaves off in any old way.
The snow is cold and very white,
Not fun if you get frost bite.
The weather can sometimes be hot,
You could get a tan or not
And so the seasons come and go
Bringing sun and wind, rain and snow.

James Paterson (11)
St Bede's School, Cambridge

THE LEOPARD

The leopard ran for its dinner
Pounce
It caught something.
The leopard tore the prey open
Chomp, chomp
Blood was dripping
From the leopard's teeth
Like a spoon of runny red jam
Red round his mouth
Like the sun fading away
The leopard licked the blood from around his lips
Slurp.

Anna McNamara (11)
St Bede's School, Cambridge

A GLIMMER OF HOPE

Feeling so small
In the depth of it all,
The silence and stillness
Of night.
An endless trace
Of night lights in space,
Brighten the darkness with white.
A magical sprinkle
Of pin pricks that twinkle,
Dusting a black canvas
With paint,
The stars in the evening
Watch our turning globe grieving -
A planet that's made many mistakes.
As the sun keeps on burning,
The world is still turning -
We're just the missing link,
To an Earth that could cope,
Without war - there is hope.
If people could just stop
And think.

Louise Pigott (14)
St Bede's School, Cambridge

MY DARK ANGEL

Black as jet,
Dark and mean,
Silently descends,
On wings of silk.

Black as a shadow,
Fly up to Heaven,
And stars up above,
With a silent cry.

A dark angel,
Yet white as snow,
You are one for sorrow,
In this nest of magpies.

Becky Wright (14)
St Bede's School, Cambridge

INDEPENDENCE

Lying in my bed
At peace with all elements
No knock at the door.

My home is my castle
Impregnable all around
The entrance is mine.

A place of safety
Where I may enjoy comfort
Only peace reigns here.

Here I find stillness
Where outside is turbulence
So danger could lurk.

But outwards I must
To discover and explore
For the world awaits.

Danger is a spice
To draw me from my haven
Into new freedoms.

Echoes of the past
These are a memorial
To independence.

Owen Sanderson (14)
St Bede's School, Cambridge

TIME...

Time is around us whatever we do,
It means such a lot to me and you,
Its constant use is our preference,
However time is merely a reference.

As we live on the Earth while it moves around,
Time makes us feel safe and sound.
Knowing where we have to be,
And what time we have free.

Time is measured in different ways,
Hours, months, years and days,
These time machines are not actual,
But to us everything is 'satisfactual.'

The past was there ... we know that was real,
But where did it begin, is that such a big deal?
The present arrives but is quickly gone,
We assume there's a future but are we wrong?

So in fact time doesn't exist,
It's a reference that we cannot resist,
We use it to make us feel secure,
Happy, safe and reassured.

Elizabeth Cameron (14)
St Bede's School, Cambridge

SUMMER IS A DRAGON

Summer is a dragon!
Hot flames from its mouth
Scales yellow, orange, red
Fire balls burning to the south
Flowers nod their sleepy heads.

Down it swoops from clear blue skies
Scorching the Earth as it flies by
Steamy waters, scorching sands
Fresh winds, cool rain, it wonders why?
Weary it limps across the land
Returning to its winter sleep!

Jasmin Mokarram (11)
St Bede's School, Cambridge

WAR

As I sit there watching the war
I see bombs flying
I see the children crying
Then I look even harder
And I see men dying.
I hear the guns go off
I see the smoke bombs
That make the soldiers cough.
I see the planes go overhead
I look again and see more men dead.
I see the medics working hard
I see two soldiers keeping guard.
All of this for what was said
Ten thousand plus men are dead.
Then when the smoke has cleared and gone
I hear the sound of victory from a horn
After all this I then start hearing
The sound of men and they're all cheering.
Now all the guns are quiet,
But I cannot believe I see this,
All the people in the street
Have now begun to riot!

Joe Minervino (14)
St Bede's School, Cambridge

PERFECTION

Beautiful eyes, you had beautiful eyes
Yet when I looked a little more closely
I discovered and unearthed your pain
When you looked into the mirror all you saw was fat
Yet when I looked at you all I saw was perfection.

I wanted to take the razor blade off you
Because I couldn't bare to see you hurt yourself.
You wanted me to take the razor blade from you
Because the cuts you made hurt so much
When you looked into the mirror all you saw were the scars
                                                      and the ugliness
Yet when I looked at you all I saw was perfection.

I wanted to take your pain away because I couldn't bare you thinking
                                                              you were nothing
You wanted me to take your pain away because you hated thinking
                                                                   like that
When you looked into the mirror all you saw was failure
Yet when I looked at you all I saw was perfection.

I wanted to hold you in my arms forever
Because I was scared of losing you
You wanted to hold me in your arms forever
Because you were scared of being alone
When you looked into the mirror all you saw was nothing
Yet when I looked at you all I saw was perfection.

I wish I could be with you now
But you're being lowered into the ground
All this because you wanted to be beautiful
All this because you wanted to be perfect
When you looked into the mirror you saw neither
Yet when I looked at you
I found it written all over your face.

Naomi Cave (14)
St Bede's School, Cambridge

SILENT WINGS

Midnight approaches, stealthily slipping,
Through broad, golden fields, silver and sleeping.

The shade of the night, craftily catching,
The triumph of daytime, cowering and creeping.

The silk of the nightfall, suffocates senses,
Envelopes minds with soft-spoken sentences.

And soaring above with wings all a-wavering
Silent as darkness, watching, waiting.

Dark eyes on white feathers, gazing, glimmering,
Piercing the night and through the gloom glimpsing . . .

. . . two more bead-black eyes, twinkling, twitching,
And a small furry tail, turning and twisting.

The owl breaks and flips, with motions fast and fleet,
And falls like an arrow with snowy white feet.

Maria Kaye (14)
St Bede's School, Cambridge

BEYOND THE SKIES

Earth for us is everything there is
We may know of distant planets
Twinkling stars
Other objects in the great black
However, the sky, intense, stormy and streaked with lightening
Blue, cloudless and bright
White and colourless
Is the limit for most of us.
When we think of the world it is
Starry skies, tropical paradises, sparse dry deserts,
Cold endless snow or rolling countryside of Earth
There is so much more
Sparkling pin pricks of light tell us of
Other planets, solar systems and suns.
Far beyond our knowledge are there
Other life forms, beautiful planets and more advanced technology?
Or life forms without technology?
Others who have no idea of our existence?
Some people believe that we humans
And this planet, Earth
Are everything that should live and exist.
One day we will be able to find out for ourselves
See other planets beyond our solar system
Travel at the speed of light to any destination
So is our world not enough?

Jeanette Langford (14)
St Bede's School, Cambridge

TREES

The eagle soars over the mountainous valley of green,
Bright eyes flickering in earnest and claws outstretched,
The pine marten looks up in horrified terror and flees,
A look of pure helplessness on his face is etched.

The eagle spots the scurrying animal searching for sanctuary,
And swoops down smoothly slicing the silent atmosphere,
The pine marten looking within his grasp and as ripe as a cherry,
But the thought of living keeps the stricken prey running in fear.

The eagle unleashes its terrible talons which gleam unnaturally,
The pine marten is so nearly caught but so nearly there,
The eagle seemingly has absorbed the animal's fear and energy
All hope and pride has left the pine marten, all power and flare.

But with one last effort he has made it to refuge under a tree trunk
The glittering triumph in the eagle's eye turns to ice-cold dread
                                                            as he cannot stop,
And he hits the tree awkwardly with a sickening clunk,
The pine marten sighs with the utmost relief and lies down
                                                            in a protected flop.

So please remember that trees are a source of refuge and are
                                                          protecting animal life,
Animals need them and we need them to live and breathe,
Do not cut them down and cause animals and ourselves so much strife,
Please, please, please, leave alone the trees.

Michael Niskin (13)
St Bede's School, Cambridge

THE SEASONS

Spring
In spring the snow will melt away
And gentle rain will fall
Spring flowers appear
Snowdrops, bluebells, daffodils
The trees wake up
Leaves slowly unfold
Lambs are born
They jump round in the fields
Little chicks begin to hatch
Everything is new.

Summer
In summer it is hot and dry
The sun warms you like a hot water bottle
The sky is blue, the grass is green,
Fields of yellow corn
Holidays - a lazy time.

Autumn
In autumn it gets cold and windy
The leaves start dropping off the trees
Lovely colours - red, orange
The wind will blow
The sky gets darker
Time to harvest the corn
To shelter the animals
To think about getting warm.

Winter
Winter is cold and damp and chilly
We love to wear hats and gloves and coats
Outside the ground is hard and frosty
The snow will fall,
The country is white
It is a beautiful sight.

Chris Allen (12)
St Bede's School, Cambridge

NO NORMAL DAY

The same, normal day
People going to work
Children going out to play,
Passengers were comfortable in their chairs,
World Trade Centre stood proud and tall,
Terrorists not even thinking about saying their prayers,
No one knew what was to draw near.
The plane approached
Passengers scared and full of fear,
The crash, the bang, the fire,
People in the streets running,
Injured people hoping to live, as they desire,
The number dead was already adding to large sums,
The dust was like a thick black cloud as the tower fell,
Families worried about their loved ones,
The children and friends who all stood and cried,
The working people who had died,
This for America was no normal day.

Sarah Nightingale (15)
St Bede's School, Cambridge

THE LIFE OF A STAR

In the beginning,
A nebula.
Clouds of gas,
Drifting through space.
Peaceful.

Bang - the furnaces in
Each concentrated ball
Commence their burning
Light and heat and power.
A beginning.

The furnaces keep burning
But fuel is not eternal.
The star grows large and red
Emitting more heat.
Dying.

Then - the end
Star runs on empty
Larger and larger and . . .
Boom - supernova.
End of a star.

What happens next?
Black hole or white dwarf,
Nebula or neutron,
Depends on the star's size.
A legacy.

However, in the matter,
Thrown out in the explosion,
Are the seeds of new stars
To take the old one's place.
A cycle.

Philip Bateman (13)
St Bede's School, Cambridge

HAND IN HAND

As I contemplate the future,
All that I can guarantee,
Is although I alone can tread this path,
You'll be here guiding me.

So far we've overcome life's trials,
Loved, laughed and cried,
I know this journey won't be tranquil,
But you stay steady by my side.

I meet many on my travels,
Some have become like family too,
Even though eternity wouldn't see us part,
I feel God leads me, always to you.

Walking in any direction,
You shelter me from harm,
A part of me knows the journey's end,
Will be found in your arms.

In your eyes our destination,
Is not clear, as in mine,
However your belief in me,
Trusts you will understand in time.

We set out with a pledge,
That no matter what life lends,
Just as we began,
We will end this as friends.

Rebecca Clarke (14)
St Bede's School, Cambridge

THE SPELL

Hubble, bubble,
Toil and trouble,
Fire burn and
Cauldron bubble.

An ear of a cat and
The wing of a bat,
Some blood of a lion,
The rust of red iron,
Add a touch of toad skin
Now we may begin.

Hubble, bubble,
Toil and trouble,
Fire burn and
Cauldron bubble.

Add an adder's tongue
And a dead man's thumb,
The dragon's hearts
My favourite part,
Put all this together and now it's a lotion
The final touch is to make it into a potion.

Hubble, bubble,
Toil and trouble,
Fire burn and
Cauldron bubble.

A lizard's foot
And some dusty soot,
A baby's eye
And a chicken's thigh,
Let them decay
Now we can say!

Hubble, bubble,
Toil and trouble,
Fire burn and
Cauldron bubble.

Sophie Lambert (11)
St Bede's School, Cambridge

FULL CIRCLE

The time ticks by
The seasons pass,
The year runs through
From courageous Capricorn, who in the winter months is born.

As spring arrives
Snow melts away,
Trees start to blossom
And self-willed Aries holds his sway.

When summer speeds in
Sun burns in the sky,
Flowers in full beauty
While caring Cancer smiles on high.

The nights draw in
The darkness falls,
The leaves are gold, red and brown
As secretive Scorpio looks down on an autumn world.

The time ticks by
The year runs through,
Back to courageous Capricorn
The seasons pass.

Oliver Worth (14)
St Bede's School, Cambridge

A Gentler Fight

The early morning mist lay across the silent lake
And the pale sun rose to light the day.

The man and the boy hunched over their rods
Both pairs of eyes trained on crimson floats.

Their prey was there beneath the glassy surface
Cautiously searching the depths for food.

This was not like the battle the man had fought before
In a faraway land of mud and decay.

Where man and boys stood hunched in the trenches
With all their eyes trained on crimson fields.

Their prey was there over the coils of barbed wire
Quietly waiting for the enemy to come.

He remembered his thoughts on that distant day
As his tired eyes fell on the crimson stains.

This was not the place for frightened boys
To learn how to fight and die.

Their hands were not for those grey, heavy guns
But to cradle a fishing rod of cane.

To sit and cast their silvery lines
Whilst the sun paints an evening crimson sky.

Thomas Lovell (13)
St Bede's School, Cambridge

The Sun

The sun is torrid, like burning bread,
Shining brightly above my head,
In the sky like a ball of fire,
Burning for us to admire.

The sun's getting lower near the horizon,
Orange, yellow and fiery crimson.
Finally now it's dropped out of view,
To be seen again in the morning dew.

Claire Thompson (13)
St Bede's School, Cambridge

A WAY OF LIFE

An orphaned infant, left alone,
Shivering and starving, without a home.
Fearfully weeping tears of despair,
Crying out because it is not fair.

An elderly lady, virtually dead,
Lying helplessly in a hospital bed.
No relatives present at her final breath,
As she proceeds on her way to death.

A homeless individual, searching the street,
There is nowhere to stay and nothing to eat.
Wrapped only in a blanket on a cold winter's night,
They dream for a way to put things right.

A forlorn family, living in third world poverty,
Yearns to exist like you and me.
A way of life, a major flaw,
The destitute community requires so much more.

A family to comfort us when things get tough,
A place to shelter so we don't sleep rough.
Possessing a life of abundance and health,
We all should be grateful for our wealth.

Rachel Lister (14)
St Bede's School, Cambridge

FIRE

Gently it flickers, lighting up the room,
Suddenly it leaps and then *boom!*
The fire has started, racing around,
Crash! Things break and fall to the ground.
It spreads out like eagles' wings,
It dances around setting light to things.
The sparks fly out orange, yellow, red.
Then it reaches over to the bed.
Oh no! The bed has gone up in flames.
It's like a lion never been tamed.
The heat is unbearable, like a sea of boiling water,
It's smashed the picture of the old man's daughter!
The sound of sirens coming down the road,
All the water in there must be a heavy load.
Splash! The water spurts from the pipe,
Making the house as dark as night.
Only ashes are left, nothing else remains,
Except for the candle with no flickering flames.
'It's all out now,' a fireman said,
'The whole house now is completely dead.'

Heather Lee (13)
St Bede's School, Cambridge

BUTTERFLIES

Butterflies go fluttering by,
On coloured wings that catch the eye.
On wings of orange and silvery blue,
On wings of golden yellow too.
Butterflies floating in the air,
Making homes almost anywhere:

The rainforest, field and prairie land,
On mountain tops and desert sand.
If winter brings the cold and snow,
To warmer climates, off they go.
Returning home the following spring,
Beautiful butterflies on the wing.

Jessica Marshall (13)
St Bede's School, Cambridge

METAMORPHOSIS

Bombs are flying, falling everywhere
Dust and debris fill the air.
There's nothing we can do, nothing we can say,
Which will make these tragedies go away.
Lives are lost and dreams are taken,
When will this world awaken?
Open its eyes to the misery and pain
Then maybe we can live again,
Without the nightmares, without the fear.
Without wondering if death is near,
In a world without hatred or guns and wars
Where people abide by all of God's laws.
It's a dream so perfect, can it possibly come true?
If we stick together we'll get through.
We'll have a world where all are free,
And can live together in unity.
There'll be no more wars and no more fighting
Mankind's flame is re-igniting.

Holly Marshall (14)
St Bede's School, Cambridge

THE GREATEST OF ALL IS LOVE

Now is the time for giving
Giving whatever you can,
Whether you're rich or poor
You can give your all
And the greatest of all is love.

It can be big, it can be small,
It is peaceful and it is calm,
It's loud and it's quiet,
It's kind and it's loyal,
It's the greatest of all, it's love.

Whether you're tall or short,
Skinny or fat,
There is one thing we all have
And there's one thing we all need,
And that's the greatest of all, it's love.

Through times of hardship and trouble,
One thing will survive,
Through wars and battles,
That one thing survives,
That's the greatest of all, that's love.

Stephanie Allum (14)
St Bede's School, Cambridge

HAZY HORIZONS

I gaze out over the hazy horizon,
Out towards the crystal sea.
In the distance dolphins are dancing
Without a care, unlike you or me.

Today in the world there's talk of war,
Thoughts of anger and deeds of hate,
Today in the world we seek revenge,
Let people forgive, before it's too late.

Nikki Jackson (11)
St Bede's School, Cambridge

HALLOWE'EN

The rustling of leaves on Hallowe'en night,
The shouts and screams of the wind,
Then suddenly a scary face, like a stormy night,
Glinted in the moonlight.
His eyes were flickering like a flame,
As he glided over the plain,
I was stiff with fear,
I could not run.
Then the phantom appeared in front of me,
Then there were two and then three,
From the undergrowth a goblin appeared,
He chased me around and around again,
In the forest and in his den.
I ran into a clearing and he stopped in his tracks,
As he saw werewolves coming in packs,
I hid from them as they ran by,
As they took off after the goblin,
I glanced at the moon it was full,
As it fell to the horizon,
Dawn was coming,
And they were going, away,
Until next Hallowe'en.

Steven Kylstra (11)
St Bede's School, Cambridge

Have You Ever Been Homeless?

Have you ever been homeless?
Where you're so alone it hurts inside
And where you feel invisible to the public eye.
Have you ever been homeless?
Where you're so hungry any food will do,
And the nights are so cold you barely pull through!
If you haven't been homeless
Have you ever passed them by?
Ate a guilty meal,
Or heard their cry!
Have you lent a listening ear
Lent a shoulder to cry on,
Protection from fear.
Can you honestly say you care enough
To stop by them and share your stuff?
Now, have you ever thought
Will I ever be homeless?

Lindsay Brand (13)
St Bede's School, Cambridge

Dream Of The Austrian Private

He says 'They will bow to our might.'
He says 'Alone we are nothing, together we are one.'
He says 'Victory shall be ours.'
What do we do? We agree.

He says 'We are the superior race.'
He says 'Our enemies are inferior.'
He says 'Perfection shall be ours.'
What do we do? We believe.

He says 'The Jews must disappear.'
He says 'They contaminate us.'
He says 'You will kill them.'
What do we do? We destroy.

He says 'It is time for war now.'
He says 'Follow me.'
He says 'We shall rule the world.'
What do we do? Surrender.

Chris Chapman (14)
St Bede's School, Cambridge

MY IDEA OF HEAVEN

Resting on the sea,
Let the current sweep you,
Clear spring air, let it engulf you,
Drifting between the trees.

Sunshine beaming,
The bright rays dispersing,
Wispy clouds parting,
Doom and gloom immersing.

Warm summer rain,
Beating the water rhythmically,
Rolling hills, towering majestically,
Sweet mist, feeling no pain.

I wish this dream were real,
My idea of heaven, so surreal.

Rebecca Saunders (13)
St Bede's School, Cambridge

My Homeland

Mist covered moors with a strong breeze and never-ending rain
The laughter of many forgotten friends
This is how I remember my birthplace, my homeland.

It's been nearly five years since I last set foot there
I remember my last day as if we never left
The sun was shining brightly, high up in the sky.

There was a hectic rush to make sure we had packed everything
The neighbours that remained said farewell
And within a few minutes we were gone, possibly never to return.

Although I left upon that day
Some might say that a part of me
Will live there forever.

Richard Griffiths (14)
St Bede's School, Cambridge

The Mountain Will Not Bow

The mountain stands alone, for it time never ends
Lightning strikes, the sky bursts forth, and from it all hell descends.
The wind rips through the valleys, the trees crack as they fall,
But the mountain stands alone, unscathed and nothing stands as tall.
Again the heavens open up and lightning scars the sky,
And winds beat the mountain side as hard as they may try.
But no matter how the wind and hail crashes upon the ground,
The mountain stands alone and never makes a sound.
With one last burst of energy, the wind suddenly came alive
And hit the mountain with such force, none other would survive.
But the mountain stood alone and strong, just as it does now,
Because no matter how much the wind may howl,
                        the mountain will not bow.

Kyle Payne (13)
St Bede's School, Cambridge

THE FORTUNE TELLER

Who wants to know their future anyway?
Who wants to know who they will marry or how long their life line is?
If someone tells you you are going to die and how long you will live for
What are you supposed to do?
Say you don't believe it?
Ignore it?
Yes.
I will make my own fortune
My own plans
I will live each day to the full
And occupy my mind with the present
Rather than the future,
With living
Rather than dying.
I will be true to myself
Not to people who think they know me better than myself.

Ruth Mullett (14)
St Bede's School, Cambridge

THE SEA

The sea is like me,
Why?

It gets calm at night,
But if I had a nightmare then the sea
Would toss its waves up high just like I would my bedcovers.

Oh the sea is just like me
It strokes the sand with its great, big hand,
Just like me when I stroke a dog or a cat.

Yes, the sea is definitely just like me.

Charlotte Gutsell (12)
St Bede's School, Cambridge

A Penance

Setting off
This is my goal and I'm excited,
It's not too steep and I'm not tired,
I can see the top and the adrenaline rushes through my body
It's a long way now, though I can't wait.
It's fresh up here, there are happy faces on their way down
I'm determined to keep on going and I won't look back.

The top
It's quiet up here, there aren't many people
There's nothing up here,
Only the view that I daren't look down at.
Too cold to feel a sense of achievement,
Too anxious about the steep journey down.

Going down
It's misty and I'm exhausted.
Fear sinks in as rocks move from beneath my feet
How many times have I fallen now?
My hands are thick with mud as are my shoes
Where I have tried to save myself.
Too scared to feel embarrassed
All that is in my mind is being safe on the ground,
There's no choice,
I must keep going there's no other way down.
Slowly, but slowly I see that I've come halfway
I'm slightly reassured, no thought to take in my beautiful surroundings
I'm nearly at the bottom now
Though all that I feel is tired.

Down at last
I look up in amazement, look how far I've come
It takes a while for what I've done to sink in
I feel overwhelmed with a sense of achievement
Seeing the top of Croagh Patrick, Ireland's holy mountain
Was for me an experience to be had
I am glad I saw my pilgrimage through.

Kimberley Muranyi (14)
St Bede's School, Cambridge

THE ALLEY CAT

The lone black cat stalks slowly down the dimly lit alleyway
Crash, bang
He pounces onto the wooden fence and gazes down suspiciously
With a graceful leap he's back on the cold, black tarmac
He hisses and arches his back as the brown and white tabby cat creeps
               round the corner
Drawing out his magnificent claws as they shine like diamonds
                and cut like swords
He lashes out and the tabby, doesn't see it coming
She knows he means business and backs off quickly licking her wound
Still hissing the black cat patrols the edge of his territory before leaping
             onto the dustbin and sitting up proudly
Rummaging through he finds a week old fish head and devours it still
               basking in his glory
His territory is now safe, he stalks back home through
               the moonlit streets
To a roaring fire and sprawls himself out at the bottom of Amy's bed.

Alison Lygo (14)
St Bede's School, Cambridge

WAR

They fight, they destroy,
There is no turning back,
Bang, he is dead,
Lifeless body on the dreaded floor,
No one cares,
Innocent victim,
No one cares,
Who will be next?
No one cares,
Remains a mystery,
Kick out of killing,
Glory out of injustice,
Beat it, fight it,
Make sure, no more,
Victims dying,
Relatives crying,
All we ask is,
Stop (please!)

Alice Matthews (13)
St Bede's School, Cambridge

THE SUN

The sun is a fiery ball
Whizzing high and low
Flying all around
East to west.

Successfully soaring over our heads,
Unusually cloudy and foggy
Now it is glorious sunshine.

Morgan Howarth (12)
St Bede's School, Cambridge

ARCADE

Buzzing with excitement
Bright, fluorescent lights
Can't wait to get there
Start to run . . .
Games
Looking at everything
Need money
Crowded with teenagers
Cha-cha-cha-ching
Shoot-'em-ups
Action-packed
Die, die, die!

Javan Hirst (11)
St Bede's School, Cambridge

GEMINI

You and I,
Hopelessly entwined,
By birth and foetal ties.

Undivided,
Not 'you' and 'me',
But an eternal 'we'.

Hopes and dreams we share,
Fear and even despair,
Bound together as one.

Reuben Mashford (14)
St Bede's School, Cambridge

I Don't Know You Anymore

It's been a year since I left you
But there's still pain in my heart.
I felt it was for the best
We just drifted apart.

I see you every time I close my eyes
You were my world, you completed me.
Without you I feel only half a person,
Living in a world that's half empty.

Seasons have changed,
The leaves are beginning to fall.
It ended so badly,
I just couldn't call.

You meant so much to me,
We were more than just best friends.
That made it so much harder,
But I knew it had to end.

We were both so young and innocent,
It was foolish to think it could last,
And now I realise,
I've been living in the past.

And then I saw you the other day,
With somebody new.
And I laughed as I realised,
I've gotten over you.

Claire Osbourn (14)
St Bede's School, Cambridge

5TH NOVEMBER

It's the 5th November, the sky is on fire,
Crashing, banging, swirling in the moonlight,
Loud and whizzing noises echoes in my ears,
Babies and children crying loudly,
The night feels eerie.

The bonfire is lit,
Guy Fawkes looks sad as he starts to burn,
The barbecue is raging,
The hot dogs are still on their stands
The night feels eerie.

Sparklers are jumping from hand to hand,
My mum's shouting,
'Don't burn your hands.'
Grandad is laughing and sounds like a giant,
The night feels eerie.

Babies are sleeping and no one is crying,
The fireworks are over,
The fire is low,
The hot dogs are eaten
The night feels eerie.

As I lie resting in my bed,
Mumbled sounds pass me by,
The night is silent
Time has flown by,
Oh! How the night is eerie,
On the 5th November.

Frances Hall (11)
St Bede's School, Cambridge

THE NIGHT SKY

The sky is like a good friend,
You can always rely on it to return and it is always there.
At night, up in the murky black,
All you can see are the stars shining brightly
And the magical moon glowing a transfixing blue.
When people think of the moon it seems so far away,
But when you look up at the big, blue shape
You almost feel as if you could touch it with the tip of your finger.
In the night sky the stars are dotted around like small pearl beads
On a large, black, velvet cape of wonderment.
If you are constantly looking at the moon,
And the endless galaxies of stars,
And the shining blue object in the middle
All of your problems just seem to fade away,
And you end up all on your own staring at the dark sky.
The mysterious sky at night provides young and old people
With hopes and dreams of flying into space.
In the velvet cape you can imagine floating around
No noise, not anyone else,
Just you and the murky, black, velvet cape of mystery,
Magic and confusion.

Jenny Warnes (14)
St Bede's School, Cambridge

WIND

The wind blows north, south, east and west
Loud like a train
Dancing with the rain.

The wind blows north, south, east and west
It's always there
It can hide like a bear.

The wind blows north, south, east and west
It can howl
It can growl wherever it wants.

The wind blows north, south, east and west
All through the night
Till fresh morning light.

Charlotte Randles-Mills (11)
St Bede's School, Cambridge

FIREWORKS

Fireworks, all different colours, red, green, blue, yellow, gold and silver
So quiet as they sit ready for take-off, unlit but ready
The enormous bonfire crackles and sparks fly up
No one notices, they are all looking at the firework
                                                        which begun to fizz,
Then suddenly *whoosh, bang, crash,* up it goes crackling like a gun,
Now lots of little ones go up, silent until crack, crash, bang,
                                                        they explode in colour,
More banging, booming into the black night sky
Then the Catherine wheel whizzing faster and faster until it's nothing
                                                        but a blur,
It explodes in colour shooting off flecks of colour like sparkles
                                                        off the grind stone,
It spins slower and slower until it's only a little ring of sparks
                                                        then it dies
Fireworks finished and the bonfire is extinguished,
                                                    it's over until next year.

Jeremy Badley (12)
St Bede's School, Cambridge

OUR PERFECT LOVE

Like a gentle breeze upon a brand new day
Your love for me is perfect, in every single way.
The way you make me feel inside whenever you are near
Makes me realise how much I need you to be here.

Like a flower needs the rain, to make it grow up tall,
I need you in winter, spring, summer or fall.
Wherever you may go, I am sure to be there,
To show how much I really love you and show how much I care.

We are like one of a kind.

Two lovers, hard to find.

We'll never be apart,

For you're always in my heart.

Vanessa Hunt (13)
St Bede's School, Cambridge

THE JOURNEY

You've planned this journey for weeks and weeks,
Packing and buying the necessities and preparing the luxuries.

Scampering around in the hectic rush as the last few weeks approach
Making sure that everything is ready
And that nothing is left out.

And then the final day arrives,
Becoming all excited you place everything into the car
All neatly and alright
You're off!

Paul Johnson (13)
St Bede's School, Cambridge

THERE ONCE WAS A MAN

There once was a man, a simple man,
Who lived in the land of Israel.
He won no awards, no commendations,
But the people, they all followed Him.

He taught of caring, a world of love,
Said things no one else would dare say.
But He captured the minds, the hearts of the few,
With stories that showed them a point.

There were a few men, some cruel men
Who wanted Him out of their way.
They felt afraid of His powerful words
So they plotted and schemed against Him.

For some time things remained silent,
Not a word was heard about Him.
Until one warm evening just after a meal,
They came to take Him away.

His friends left Him to be taken away,
They left Him to be put to His death.
He was spat at, He was whipped and beaten,
And finally judgement was passed.

He was pulled in front of the governor,
'You shall die' he said and washed his hands.
So they took Him away, nailed Him to a cross
Hanging between two sinners.

There once was a man, a simple man
Who said from the cross on the hill.
'Father forgive, they know not what they do,'
Jesus cried, 'I give you my life.'

Robert Jackson (14)
St Bede's School, Cambridge

YAKASHOUMIES

Under the ocean where the fair winds blow,
And the sunlight surfs the waves,
The darkness lurks in the swell of the sea
And sunbathes in watery caves.
All day through the cold, black night,
Alone they travel as one
And in the darkness under the tide,
They're idle till their work is done.
Evil by name and evil by nature,
Their gaping mouths held shut,
Consuming joyfully all that is bad,
To quiet their gurgling guts.
So under the ocean where the fair winds blow,
And the sunlight surfs the waves,
Remember the malice, cruelty and fear,
For now you know . . . Yakashoumies are near.

Jennie Johnson (13)
St Bede's School, Cambridge

THE BARN OWL

The white, graceful barn owl
Sitting like a shape in moonlight
On the time-blackened beams
Still and quiet as a church mouse
Suddenly a rustle in the grass
Wings like moonlight blades
Cutting through the night
A tussle,
A pounce,
Silence.

Benjamin Dixon (13)
St Bede's School, Cambridge

MY HOLIDAY

Gleaming sun shining down on the golden sand
    Like a ball of fire.

Big, tall trees which are green and brown
    Standing tall and proud.

Little, small island in the middle of the sea
    So quiet and small like a little round pea.

Big, blue sea with starfish floating on the top
    And sea horses swimming around in the sea.

Ships come in and trucks ruin trees
    Making everything dull and not as pretty as it used to be.

Big houses ruin wildlife making everything quiet
    No noise except for cars.

All is left in the big, blue sea which is green and dirty.

Tad Cook (12)
St Bede's School, Cambridge

WIND

Moving swiftly through the air
Howling, howling everywhere
Sometimes it can be quite mild
Even to a baby child.
It fills the space around us
And sometimes creates a fuss.
The wind can be scary
And sometimes it's like a fairy.
Yes, it is the wind.

Alistair Campbell (12)
St Bede's School, Cambridge

AUTUMN

Autumn arrives, the nights draw in,
The leaves fall off the trees,
The wind blows, the trees move,
The leaves flutter to the ground,
They make a carpet of golden brown,
So soft to walk upon,
Leaves are changing all the time,
Yellow, orange, golden brown
Rain follows pitter-patter as it hits the ground,
The rain changes to snow so quickly,
So white, so cold, so silent,
So hurry home,
To fires bright,
So warm, so cosy, throughout the night,
I now miss autumn,
So clean and so fresh,
With leaves that are golden,
And the air is so fresh,
How I miss autumn,
And the time I had to play.

Christopher Thurston (11)
St Bede's School, Cambridge

WHAT YOU GET FROM THE TUMBLE DRIER

You may call me a weirdo
But I don't really care
Except in my spare time
I mess with a ball of hair.

I twing it and twang it
And make it into a ball
You might think I'm stupid
But I never get bored at all.

I mess with it in my school
But no one seems to mind
And I can make my ball bigger
Using anything I find.

Simon Pettit (11)
St Bede's School, Cambridge

DREAMS

Rolling hills
In a tumbling land,
Playing on the beach
In the silky sand.

A smile on your friend's face
Like a warm summer's day
A crow laughing,
As horrible things to you they say.

Dreams of the food
You had today,
Or a magical world
With the flowers of May.

Dreams are all in a world
Of sleep,
But privately yours in
Your thoughts down deep.

Funny ones, sad ones
And scary ones too.
They could be anything,
Imagine the perfect one
. . . for *you!*

Olivia Pinnock (11)
St Bede's School, Cambridge

THE WITCHES AND THEIR CAULDRON

They gathered around their heart of worship
Adding evil, envy and poison
    Froth and foam,
    Burn and bubble,
    Make this potion cause lots of trouble.

Blind man's toe and ear of bat,
Dragon's blood and fang of cat
    Froth and foam,
    Burn and bubble,
    Make this potion cause lots of trouble.

It stood on its legs, hissing with delight,
They cackled cruelly and chorused . . .
    Froth and foam,
    Burn and bubble,
    Make this potion cause lots of trouble.

Unicorn's hair and beauty within
Sugar, spice and acid sin
    Froth and foam,
    Burn and bubble,
    Make this potion cause lots of trouble.

Their familiars stared with glowing eyes
Their heads filled with secret lies
    Froth and foam,
    Burn and bubble,
    Make this potion cause lots of trouble.

The witches' eyes were malicious and staring,
Their pupils reflecting the dancing flames
   Froth and foam,
   Burn and bubble,
   Make this potion cause lots of trouble.

Their deed was done, the damage everlasting
An electric flash and they had gone.

Julian Dickson (12)
St Bede's School, Cambridge

THE GAME

The wind whistles through the long, dry grasses
Of the Savannah.
The sky twinkles with a thousand bright stars
Like windows into Heaven.
The moon beams down on the quiet scene of tranquillity.
She stalks
Through the undergrowth
The sound of her ragged breath in her ears
The wildebeest drink at the pool
So still, unaware
She crouches . . .
She sprints . . .
She pounces.
A shriek cuts through the still night air
She played the game of life and death
And she won.

Rachel Moseley (14)
St Bede's School, Cambridge

FIONA'S FINGER

Fiona's finger
Had a mind of its own
Like a worm
Searching food,
Poking and prodding
In the
Strawberry trifle,
Jelly,
Ice cream,
Until it found
The pile high,
Chocolate,
Sponge with cream
And then like
A submarine
It plunged in
Exploring the depths
It emerged and
Found its way to
Fiona's mouth.

Maybe it doesn't have
A mind of
Its own
After
All!

Holly Gowler (11)
St Bede's School, Cambridge

GREENS

Never eat your mangy greens
If your parents like to be really mean
Sprouts and broccoli, disgusting foods
Just sulk and huff and be in a mood.

But when you get to your parents' age
You'll have your own kids by that stage
So feed them ugly, healthy things
Then you can sit back and watch 'em cringe!

Ellis Winster (12)
Sawston Village College

DREAMING

I am walking,
I am talking,
I am moving,
I am staying silent,
I am lying still.

A dreamer's mind
Flashes images
Of people,
Of places,
Of past.

A dreamer floats
Unconscious of the world
Not aware of outside
You know you are dreaming
But you cannot escape.

You travel miles
You travel centuries
You are this person
Or you are that
You are anyone

You are dreaming.

Joanne Farley (13)
Sawston Village College

THE BLANK PAGE

A poem that I wrote when I couldn't think what to write.

I stare down at the blank page
An empty space waiting to be written on
Or maybe it will stay as it is,
White and clean.
Maybe writing will never spread to cover it
Who can say?
Maybe it will end up as part of a story
Or even a letter or a poem
Maybe the writing will bring happiness to all who read it,
Or maybe it will spread sadness and devastation.
Who knows?

Rowena Smith-Lamkin (13)
Sawston Village College

SLIPPING AWAY

At his bedside
All was still
He was calm
And very pale.
I felt so cold
And isolated.
I stared at him
He looked at me
I could feel it
He was leaving me.
I held his hand
And. . .
He took his
Last breath . . .

Melody Tomlin (14)
Sawston Village College

AMERICAN NIGHTMARE

Everything is gone.
Loved ones lost.
In return - nothing,
Only a snow of ashes left behind.
Anger,
Hatred,
Pity and sadness.

The brave men work by sun and moon,
Trying to save those trapped beneath.
Stars shine bright,
But nothing helps
That growing pain of heartache.

Helen Wragg (13)
Sawston Village College

THE WHALE

A silent blue shadow
gliding, gently through the ocean
as old and wise as God himself
graceful, quiet,
slowly swimming through the sea
singing his gentle song.
Agile, untouchable
king of all the creatures
unchanged since the dawn of time
he is the soul of the ocean
he is
       the
              whale.

Maria Reali (11)
Sawston Village College

THE NEW YORK DEVASTATION - THE RESCUE TEAM ARRIVES

We arrive at the scene
It's horrible
It's shocking.

I look up where the Twin Towers stand
Both ablaze
And billowing smoke
From their gaping wounds,
Where each plane has hit
Destroyed is each and every item inside
It's horrible
It's shocking.

Immediately
We start the search
We enter and help
Evacuate the weak
And dying building
Of all the people inside
It's horrible
It's shocking.

One person
On the seventy-fourth floor
Unable to use his legs,
I lift him over my shoulder
I carry him down
To the ground floor.
He's safe
He's living
Before I have a chance
To go back inside
The first tower starts to collapse
'Run!' is the first thing that is said
So that is what we are doing.

We're running
Not stopping
The ominous cloud of dust
Follows us very closely.
It swallows people on its way
Suffocating them, they cannot breathe
They're choking
They're dying.

Now, because of all the dust
Our work has been postponed
We have to wait for it to clear
We have to leave survivors trapped
Underneath all the rubble
Leave them for many hours,
Maybe for a day
Until the dust has cleared
Nothing can be done
New York is in devastation
It's horrible,
It's shocking.

Max Appleton (13)
Sawston Village College

I LIKE THE NIGHT

I sit in the park all day 'til night,
The sun fades away 'til there isn't any light.
Will I go home, I don't know I might,
But I enjoy sitting in the park, alone in the night.

Donielle Brymer (13)
Sawston Village College

DISASTER

I had heard the sickening crash
As clearly as my mother's sobs in the next room
I had seen the terrified people running from the disaster
Never have I seen such indescribable sights
As the cloud of dust went up I knew families would never be the same.
Little did I know one of those thousands of families would be mine.

When I heard the news of my father
My stomach wrenched
My head felt cloudy
My throat felt dry and itchy
But most of all my heart felt like someone had grabbed hold of it
And was pulling it apart.

I had never felt so much pain
It tore at my flesh
I couldn't control myself
I had to scream
It was bubbling up inside me
Through my stomach, up my throat
Out through my mouth.

No one looked at me
They were feeling the same but screaming inside
I hope my father had felt no pain
Maybe one of those screams I heard belonged to my father
Why would anyone do this?
This cold, cruel act of evil
I now ask you: could you do something so evil?
If so, may God have mercy.

Megan Saunders (12)
Sawston Village College

THE MONKEY MAN

With a face like a monkey's in a zoo
He sits and sits on the station chair
And remembers
He thought back to when he sat there at the age of four
As his father got on the train
He remembered the last kiss
The last time he saw that smile
So he went to live by the railway line
And sit and sit.
His eyes now sunk into his mask of tragedy.
His forehead was crumpled like a stormy sea
On a large melon-sized head.
The monkey man sits and sits on the station bench
His body was hunched like a wilting plant
And I don't wonder why
For he has had no food or drink
For a week or more.
His small fragile fingers fumble with a roll of tobacco
The only thing that keeps him alive!
A boy like you or I walked by
And saw the man alone
But showed no sign of sorrow
Just laughed and carried on.
The boy came back with a group of friends
And threw pennies at him, hard.
He should not sit there alone and be teased
For he is just like you or I
But there the monkey man sits and sits
And the train comes down the line.

Susannah Bangham (12)
Sawston Village College

A Strike To The Heart

The beginning, shock,
An overwhelming disbelief
Watching, the plane crashing again and again
The murder of thousands.

Hopelessness too far away
But still feeling that fear and hatred
One country, two towers, four hijacked planes
So many people affected.

Now anger, disgust,
The constant fear of certain war.
The many tales of missing people, never found
A planned disaster, pure evil.

War can't be the answer,
An easy solution to a difficult problem
It's just revenge, a way to kill
And history repeats and repeats and repeats.

Catherine Nobes (14)
Sawston Village College

School Is . . .

School is an evil prison for convicted children.
School is a horrible headache of numbers and letters.
School is the fiery underworld of tired children and trapped souls.
School is a labyrinth and teachers are raging minotaurs.
School is a hectic ants' nest of pupils working.
School is a sticky web catching unaware children in its learning.
School is a fearsome jungle, children are the prey.
School is the mean judge, children are defendants.
School is waiting and praying for home time.

Sam Chequer (12) & Chris Evans (11)
Sawston Village College

INSIDE A GIRL'S HEAD

There is a place where they listen to gossip and talk about boys,
A place where they giggle, laugh and make lots of noise.
They fear all spiders especially ones that are big and hairy,
But spiders think girls are ten times more scary.
They love their shops and want the most expensive tops.
Some of them are so dense
They'd climb a glass fence to see the other side.

They hate football,
Though it's so cool, they'd rather chill out in a swimming pool.
They always ask 'Does my bum look fat?'
They know the answer they want to get back.
So I feel like saying 'Yes!
You're a total mess.'
That's about all
And as a warning,
They can get as mad as a bull.

Michael Ford (12)
Sawston Village College

TEACHER

A teacher is a devil locking you in Hell.
A teacher is a witch who puts you in a trance.
A teacher is a monster covered in a skin.
A teacher *can* be kind but strict as well.
A teacher is a relation who helps you live your life.
A teacher is a person who breaks free at night.
A teacher is a tamer who calms children down.
A teacher is one of a million stars teaching others.
A teacher has feelings like everyone else,
A teacher is, well, a teacher!

Lucy Deeming (11)
Sawston Village College

... AGAINST THE WORLD

Evil,
Portrayal of uncontrollable upset
Anger,
Vehicle transformed to weapon.
Helplessness.
Choices: jump or burn?
Suicide,
People like us, unable to even imagine
Blood
Rescue efforts now just not,
Efforts
Civilised societies bonding
War.
Suspect: Bin Laden
Wanted,
Dead or alive.

Sophie Maloney (13)
Sawston Village College

THE EARTH

The Earth is a sphere, suspended in space.
The Earth is changing day by day.
The Earth is a mix of colours and beliefs.
The Earth is a mix of sadness and joy.
The Earth is a mix of rich and poor.
The Earth is a mix of birth and death.
The Earth is a mix of starvation and greed.
The Earth is a mix of loneliness and friendship.
The Earth is ours to protect and care for
The Earth is an amazing place.

Peter Martin
Sawston Village College

TWIN TRAGEDY

The floor moved as though in an earthquake
I've never known such a powerful shake,
Terror and panic were spreading fast,
I hoped this nightmare wouldn't last
Instinctively we leapt to the stairs -
All wondering 'What's happening?' 'Get out!' 'Who cares?'
We reached the ground level just in time
Was this an accident or some terrible crime?
The north tower's been hit by a plane they say
People are panicking, running away.
Another plane appears in the sky
South tower's been hit now, why, why, why?
The towers collapse, dust covers the sun -
And buildings, colleagues, friends have gone.
I think of them now, all in Heaven.

Tom Chalk (13)
Sawston Village College

HEAVEN

Heaven is . . .
A cage of love enclosed by a ball of cloud.
A drop of happiness in the pool of the afterlife.
A ball of hope in the heart of every person.
A candle in the dark that surrounds us.
A blossom of joy in the tree of who we are.
A bright sun, a silver moon and a million stars.
A beautiful dream.
A clear lake in the muddy marshland of our galaxy.
A diamond in the mine of coal.
The home of God and all His angels.

Abigail Hunt (11)
Sawston Village College

EMPTINESS

                                        Middle

Nothing

             Start   Zero

Who

            Insignificant

                          Them

Why

                 Gone

Non-existent

                                Thoughts

    You

Finish

                     Space

                                      Beginning

Us

     None.

Fraser Clark (12)
Sawston Village College

THE NIGHT SKY

I sit and watch the misty clouds race by
As they reveal the smouldering midnight sky
I gaze upon a shining, shooting star
The golden light glows softly from afar
The frosted moon sails on throughout the night
The moon beams bright with all its able might
I listen, but not the buzz of a bee,
Nor even the chink of a glistening key.
A howl of wind breaks the tranquillity
And lightning flashing on the distant sea.

Charlie Collier (11)
Sawston Village College

MY HEAD

Inside my head
There's a joker or two.
Or a scolding teacher
To punish you.

                Or a massive mouth,
                Just ready to chat.
                Or a massive microphone
                But I'm louder than that.

Or a big, burning flame
Burning tempers so red
Enough to wake anyone
Even the dead.

                Or a Homer Simpson
                Drinking Duff beer.
                Or a mischievous pixie
                Well, that is just clear.

Or listen to this
It is a bit scary,
It could be me
Being an annoying fairy.

                So this is just me
                It'll be me forever
                And will it all change?
                Ha! I think never.

Natasha DeMartino (12)
Sawston Village College

HELPLESS

My broken chest burns, like a fire crackling and spitting,
I scratch my bites from the flies that live on me.
I pull my jacket up over my unshaven face
My bible lays on my numb, bare feet
My chequered shirt ripped by the attackers
That left me for dead.
The wind blares into my large ears
It catches my breath as I whisper 'Take me away,
End this misery.'

The entrance to a car park isn't too bad
At least the rain can't taunt me here.
I curl my knees up to my chest
As the wind howls in and out of the dark passages.
My bony fingers snap like fireworks
As I run them together for heat,
My fragile legs like blades of grass
Stamped on then axed aside
To be dumped with the other rotting nobodies.

I have nothing but the shredded clothes,
That I lie awake in
The bible
That gives me my last strand of hope
I hauled myself up, using the wall as a support
I fall
Helpless.

Lucy Baglin (12)
Sawston Village College

I AM YOU, YOU ARE ME

I'm a homeless old lady
I'm out in the cold,
You're in the warm.

I'm a person
You're a person.

No one cares about us,
We are the same!

I'm unhappy,
I strain to reach happiness
I am you, you are me.

I wear rags,
I'm weak,
You wear warm, soft clothes,
You are strong.

I wish I had a husband
A house and money.
Instead,
My life is disintegrating into . . .
Nothing!
Like sugar in boiling water
I have nothing to live for.

As a child I used to dream
I would grow up rich,
But it all just shatters right here in front of me.

I am you, you are me.

Sarah Pettican (13)
Sawston Village College

RUNNING

The man sat huddled in a tight, dirty doorway
Humming an old tune to survive.
Afraid of sleeping
Afraid of staying awake
Confused
The man's feelings, nobody knows
The man's hopes, thoughts and dreams, nobody cares.

Some children came out of a restaurant
They taunted him with a fiver,
The man stared and stared
Then reached out a hand
The children laughed and ran off.

Tears struck the man's eyes like a poisonous shark,
He couldn't control his fear,
The man ran
And ran
And ran,
Abuse and laughter on his back, weighing him down.

Is there a reason to be this insane,
Yes,
It is you,
It is you,
The ones who shout abuse,
The ones who laugh and point.

John Young (12)
Sawston Village College

INSIDE A GIRL'S HEAD

Inside a girl's head
Her images of fashion and beauty
She wants to be famous
Like all those other stars
She's the richest girl in the universe
And the prettiest.

Inside a girl's head
She is ugly as hell
Spots erupting all over her face
Torturing her
She can't resist temptation -
Squeeze!

Inside a girl's head
When all adore her, all wanting
To be her friend
She's the best and loudest
All look up to her, wishing to be her
Popular!

Inside a girl's head
She's alone, so very much alone
No one there to like her
No one there to adore her
Alone with nobody to care
Lonely.

Bai-ou He (12)
Sawston Village College

REPETITION

Sea,
They glide and eat away at the mounting rocks,
The white horses canter to the water's edge.
They gracefully pick up smooth stones and fine sand,
Pushing it onto the seabeds and the shore.
Maybe it will stay that way,
Forever,
Continually repeating itself,
Over and over again.

Life,
Always the population thickening and thickening,
Continually travelling for no reason whatsoever.
It uses people to help it and uses people to break it,
And why? Why? Why does it happen to us?
Always hurting us that way,
Forever,
Continually repeating itself,
Over and over again.

William Hewson (13)
Sawston Village College

NIGHT

In the dark of the night,
far beyond Earthly light,
the sky is drowned by the dark night,
in the darkness there is moonlight,
there's a strange ghastly sight,
that will give you a fright.

Adam Marritt (13)
Sawston Village College

THE EARTH

The Earth is a ball of energy, powered by a lamp.

The Earth is a complicated planet, full of intelligent life.

The Earth is a ruthless prison, all the occupants sentenced to life.

The Earth is a metal marble amongst others pulled in by a magnetic force by the biggest, brightest marble in the pack.

The Earth is a spinning football lost in the middle of infinite space.

The Earth is a sphere nest for billions of ants.

The Earth is a roller coaster ride taking you through the ups and downs of life.

The Earth is a ball of green and blue flames, which was shot out of Hell.

The Earth is a broken piece of Heaven like a piece of fresh bread.

The Earth is a home, home to all humans, animals and insects of every kind.

Laurence Nye (11)
Sawston Village College

BLACK BLANKET!

The moon brings in the soft, black sky,
And as the stars appear,
It brings a tear to my eye

The wolf howls
And screech goes the owl
As the black blanket tucks in the land nearby!

Alex Campbell (13)
Sawston Village College

GIRLS JUST WANNA HAVE FUN!

Inside a girl's mind is a forest full of perfect things
Everything she could ever dream of
But she can't have
And yet there is a garden full of all her nightmares
And like terrible weeds they grow
Spinning around her and trapping her
Then, hundreds, thousands of gorgeous men rush by
Though only the last one stops and sets her free.
Wonderful music plays softly
As they wander into the sunset
But suddenly it ends,
Her fairy tale dream is over
The music stops playing
And the only sound is her gentle sobbing
Heartbroken
She walks again
Through fields of golden corn
She's walking through mud,
Her shadow following her all the time
Like a stalker mimicking her every move
Oh . . . but it's not mud . . . it's chocolate!
Loud, funky, dance music fills the air,
The stars turn into disco lights
And the moon is a giant mirror ball!
Forgetting all about the handsome man
All about her worries
She dances the night away
With her friends
Glitter falling from the sky
After all, boys come and go
But her friends are forever!

Harriet Richmond (12)
Sawston Village College

TOPAZ

She slinks around in style,
A show off Siamese,
A fresh stack of clothes all neat in a pile,
She'll sleep on top of them all,
In Summertime she'll sleep in the sun,
Inside or out it doesn't matter,
She misses out on all the fun,
But she doesn't care,
She'd rather be alone,
Then do a dare!

She'll link under a hand that's,
There to stroke another,
She'd rather lay down then stand,
While you fuss her around,
She'll come when there is food
And wait while in between,
It will depend on her mood
If she is to sit with you,
When Winter comes, she'll stay
In as much as she can
And when she does with who?

And then she'll come back
After her morning stroll,
Then you go off on your hack
With your horse and a friend,
While she is already sleeping
When you come back,
She hears the door SLAM and then she takes a peep . . .
But she has always been your cat!

Rebecca Pryce (13)
Sawston Village College

WHY ARE WE HERE?

In the darkness
There is a door,
Behind that door
There stands a child,
A child who hears your every thought
Who sees the hidden past,
Future,
And present.
A child who knows the world around,
Who feels the threat,
Before it exists.
A child with a mission,
A purpose,
Survive.
But even to the child from whom it seems
Nothing can be hidden
There is a question
Without an answer
Where did we come from?
Why are we here?

Megan Overend (12)
Sawston Village College

WORLD BEFORE WAR

Mummy, what was the world like
When you were just a child?
Did you live on top of the Earth?
Did creatures live in the wild?

Mummy, what colour is the sun?
What colour is the sky?
Is there really a moon up there
Or is this just a lie?

Mummy, what was the Earth like?
Did fruit really grow on trees?
What did the wind feel like?
Did you feel a summer breeze?

Mummy, will I see these things?
If I go above the ground?
What will it be like up there?
What will I surround?

Emma Hewer (14)
Sawston Village College

KNOCKING ON DEATH'S DOOR

Lying helpless in a hospital bed
Sharp needles of pain searing through my body
Faces tower above me, smiling, talking
They make me feel so small
Everything will be fine they say
Will they ever see the truth?
I want to tell them this truth
I want to say, leave me
Let me go with my dignity in tact
But I am too weak
Already too frail.
Soon I'll be nothing more than a faint heartbeat.
I need help, need to get out of this hell
I need to be at peace.
For this I need help
These faces, if they truly love me they'll help me go.
They'll stop my pain, and theirs.
They'll make it quick,
They'll put me in a better place.

Hannah Margaret Edwards (13)
Sawston Village College

HOMELESS MAN

Drink, eat, sleep, scavenge,
Eyes open, face full of boot,
Run now, carry blanket
Cackles of children who committed assault.

Walk now, walk to work,
Pretending that you have a job,
Wake up now, live in the real world,
You're scum, dust, dirt, worthless.

Walk back down the street
Not knowing what you will meet,
So is the life of a homeless man
A homeless man who has been damned
Drink, eat, sleep, scavenge,
Drink, eat, sleep, scavenge.

Martin Ball (12)
Sawston Village College

INSIDE A BOY'S HEAD

There is a river of thoughts and emotions,
A river of swirling feelings
This river flows through good and bad
This river trickles gently with great love and friendship
But is also a raging torrent of hate and fear,
And there's a dam built to keep these things inside
And this dam is built as strong as mountains
But no dam can stop a river flowing
So one day this dam will burst . . .

Danny Harris (12)
Sawston Village College

TSUNAMI

A crystal blue wave burnt pure evil,
Its order to destroy,
It rolls and rumbles and then rears over,
To watch its victims to be.

The giant wave reaches out,
Its fingers crushing what's underneath,
Triggered by an earthquake,
All existence comes to a watery death.

The wave glints in the sun as though it's studded with gems,
But then it converts into a tall monster of white froth,
A tsunami is a suicide killer
Using its life to murder others.

A crystal blue wave turned pure evil,
Its order to destroy,
Although they say it's picturesque,
I wouldn't stand and admire!

Jenny Nobes (11)
Sawston Village College

THE SEA IS . . .

A lagoon of floating velvet,
a paradise of calmness,
the waves gently rocking against the craggy rocks,
the sea slipping like a snake,
a turquoise jumper trapping the deep blue sea,
a breath of fresh air among the midday breeze,
a mermaid singing sweetly, laying upon her rock,
a dolphin dancing swiftly in the summer air.

Chloé Pantazi (11)
Sawston Village College

BLACK ISLE

Waves stampede,
Birds screech,
Towering cliffs touch the clouds
I was approaching Black Isle.

A deserted place,
Without a trace of life
Jagged rocks hide the brown sand,
Trees droop in sadness of the isle.

I creep out my small boat
Peer around
The wind howls and wails,
I tiptoe towards a wooden hut.

The wood is damp, mouldy,
Parts dropping off
Moss covering almost every part of wood
I pull open the door that is almost falling off.

I step in through the door, into the cold hut
It was filled with bones,
Big bones, small bones, all scattered around the room
Brownish coloured bones, white bones,
Bits of flesh hanging onto them.

One wall smeared with blood,
Not a bit of wood showing
It was dripping onto the bones below
Something was very wrong on this island.

I turned around and ran,
I headed towards my boat
It had gone, nothing was there
I stopped, a ghostly figure stared at me
A cold chill went through my body.

Waves stampede,
Birds screech,
Towering cliffs touch the clouds
Another dead body on Black Isle.

Alistair White (12)
Sawston Village College

DESPAIR

His face as wrinkled as a raisin
His eyes sunken in like a cave,
Slouching on the bench,
Watching the day go by.

His bones cut out of the side of his body,
His elbows as sharp as a pin,
As people walk passed they look at him,
Flinching and scuttle away.

As people look at him,
They see his blank look,
Shutting out his past life,
Blocking it with a stony face.

His only entertainment is rolling his cigarette,
And searching the streets for penny coins,
His back feels like it's going to snap,
And his fingers are bleeding and sore.

He makes his way through the park,
Making his way to his shelter,
He lies down on his cardboard bed,
And dreams of his dying day.

Johanna Yassin (12)
Sawston Village College

MOURNING FOR NATURE

When nothing is left of creation
But a concrete slab,
When radio,
Computer,
And the Internet,
Are the only words.
When whole rainforests disappear,
And the world is stripped bare,
When the sea has turned bright green,
And every animal has become extinct,
People will forget grass,
Trees,
And animals.
The feeling of the wind in your hair,
The fresh smell after a spring rainstorm,
The blue of the Mediterranean Sea,
The sand as it sticks between your toes,
The sweet taste of plums, fresh from the tree,
But not me,
I will mourn for nature
And it will live on in me.

So look after the planet or
All you'll have left,
The only memory of nature
And happiness will be me!

Clare Tubby (14)
Sawston Village College

NIGHT

The moon shines down from the glistening sky
Just like the stars, it's ever so high
The trees are like giants in the night
All the dark shadows will give you a fright.

All the creatures hustling around
Creeping speedily along the ground
Night is a time for all those to sleep
Until the alarm goes *Bleep! Bleep! Bleep!*

Iain Hyde (13)
Sawston Village College

CLOCK

Its smiley face is ticking away,
dreaming about being a grandfather clock.

Tick-Tock, Tick-Tock.

Its hands are like children's lollipop
sticks, slightly chewed up.

Tick-Tock, Tick-Tock.

Its battered design on the rim is twisting and turning,
writhing like snakes.

Tick-Tock, Tick-Tock.

Its roman numerals are like actors,
each waiting until it is their spot in the limelight,
when the hands rest on them, showing their best.

Tick-Tock, Tick-Tock.

Its ticking, like a scared child's heart beating . . .

    beating . . .
        beating . . .
            ticking . . . forever.

Maya Bienz (11)
Sawston Village College

TO A FRIEND...

You helped me find myself
When I had given up searching.

You restored faith in my existence,
When I had given up hope.

You shielded me from harm,
Despite my resentment.

You remained by my side
Although I continued to walk alone.

Your vulnerability became my strength,
Your commitment became my courage,
Your love became my salvation.

Holly-Bethe Moseley (14)
Sawston Village College

THE WOOD AT NIGHT

As the trees make a peering sound
It's hard to notice if they move around.

As they bend, incline and sway,
You don't usually hear this at day.

You don't see, its so foreboding,
It's like being blind, so unknowing.

You feel so scared, so alone,
All you can hear are the whales and groans.

Dan Matthews (13)
Sawston Village College

THE WIND

Breathing, but not alive,
And as bitter as death,
Voiceless as it cries,
Yet sound is produced,
Silently it passed by,
But you feel its presence,
Mighty and immortal,
But you smell no essence,
But like a . . .

Howl in the silent night
A whisper when you're all alone,
A shadow creeping by
Someone waiting to rise up,
The wind . . .

Hannah Kite (12)
Sawston Village College

SPACE

A black hole
Shapeless
Endless darkness
Moon shining
Stars twinkling
Millions of light years away
A dark lagoon
Black velvet studded with diamonds
A lonely space of time
New planets, waiting to be found
A cold and icy blanket covering the sky
It goes on for ever and ever.

Eleanor Tubby (11)
Sawston Village College

SOMEDAY

Someday I'll run the high roads
That are still so long and wild.

One day I'll swim the oceans
When the tide is down and mild.

Someday I'll calm the babies
That seem to always cry.

One day I'll watch the eagles
Soaring through the sky.

Someday I'll follow the footsteps
Of the people's hearts I fill.

One day I'll wipe away the tears
Of the suffering, sick and ill.

Someday I'll see the shadows
Of the people who smiled all day.

One day I'll think of Heaven
And tell them I'm on my way.

Lauren King (14)
Sawston Village College

NIGHT BLANKET

Night is like a patchwork blanket
With randomly stitched stars,
The stars are like fireflies,
Shimmering from afar.

Carefully sewn into the night
A huge silver ball
It looks a giant 10 pence piece
Shining over all

The midnight velvet blanket
Is laid softly on the world
Over every person in their bed
As they sleep all tightly curled

Stephanie Howe (14)
Sawston Village College

DREAMWORLD

Darkness descends
And the gate opens
An entrance to the world of dreams

An open portal
To a shimmery, silvery world
Birthplace of infinite dreams

An open door
To a dark, black, evil realm
A breeding ground for nightmares

A golden passage
From a radiant sphere
Of beautiful angels

A gloomy tunnel
From a corrupted globe
Of fearsome demons

Dawn breaks
And the gate swings shut
Across the entrance to the dream world.

Elizabeth Hale (14)
Sawston Village College

THE WORST THING ABOUT BEING HOMELESS

I just woke up from my cold, wet sleeping
With my matted hair down to my shoulder
In sodden smelly rags
With wet old trainers
I beg for food but no one cares
Can't get a job
Just look at me
I'm homeless and jobless
I don't want your sorrow.
I just want your coppers
Hostel turned away from me. I have no one else
Alcoholics
Evil
Shiftless baby killers
After your money
That's what people think of me.
Moneyless, foodless, jobless and homeless.

Sarah Thompson (13)
Sawston Village College

MY HEAD

In my head there are three doors each waiting to be opened
to reveal myself but I'm too scared to open them.

In my head there is a long line of forgotten homework.

In my head there is a tornado which I try to avoid
but it sucks me into a whirl of anger.

All around my head there is music to drown out the
constant shouting of my parents.

Jodi Keen (12)
Sawston Village College

HIGH FLYING

Weightless
Soaring like an eagle
Whooshing through the clouds
Peering in the windows of aeroplanes
Free as a bird
Zooming like a car
A gliding ballroom dancer

My own pilot
Sailing through the air
Faster than the Olympic runners

Then I go to land
An autumn leaf, fluttering to the ground
And then the 'thump' when I hit the ground
Ruins the silence
I'm back to roam the world.

Freya Chaplin (12)
Sawston Village College

NIGHT

The night is like a virus
Spreading through the land
Dissolving all light in its path
The dark blanket covers everything
Houses, animals, people.

We run from the darkness into the light
But it seeps in like a ghost
And makes shadows in the light.

The only thing to do is to wait till dawn.

Martyn Willis (13)
Sawston Village College

WAR ORPHAN

He sits alone in the dark,
He does not know of his past,
And he worries of what the future holds,
He knows those happy days are gone,
He feels so alone.

>He doesn't know why he's here,
>What did he do to be punished in this way?
>They speak a language he doesn't understand,
>No one ever listens to his little voice,
>He feels so alone.

He hears the noises of the war,
They all come from inside his head,
Bombs, aeroplanes, sirens the screaming,
They all come back to haunt him,
He feels so alone.

>He sees images of the war.
>His mother, the flames, death and destruction,
>The ghosts of his past,
>Every night he wakes because of a nightmare,
>He feels so alone.

He thinks about his obscure past,
And always wonders if there is a cure,
If only he could turn back time,
And he could stop this act of war,
He feels so alone.

>They all say they know how he feels,
>How they love him,
>Inside he's not so sure,
>He only needs loving, needed and protecting,
>He feels so alone.

Every night he weeps,
Every night he prays,
And every morning nothing has changed,
Just him and his only toy,
He knows he isn't wanted,
The nightmares just don't go away.

Susannah Hodge (14)
Sawston Village College

THE MOON

A guide at night
A shining light
Dazzling bright
Still and cold

                    A flashing torch
                    Beaming on my porch
                    Standing course
                    Still and cold

A dolphin curled up
A silver figure
Shiny but dusty
Still and cold

                    The end of the day
                    It comes out to stay
                    Standing calmly
                    Still and cold

A feather that's light
A feather that's white
Still and cold

Emma Cracknell (11)
Sawston Village College

IN MY HEAD

There is a bull fenced off just waiting to charge.
In my head there is a door just waiting to be opened
Although, I don't have the keys.
There is a black hole waiting to swallow me up
And I'm just holding on to an inch of reality.
When I close my eyes there is a world
Full of flowers and strange creatures touching me,
I feel safe and scared.

In my head there is a constant swirl of nagging
There is no finish or no start
Just keeps on going until the end of time.

Amber Dyer (12)
Sawston Village College

RUBBLE

I travelled here from England,
And was not expecting this.
It all happened in a blur.
The dust and smoke will clear,
But the wounds and broken families will not.
Inside the layer of smoke in the air,
Hate lingers over the city.
Fear hovers over the heads of survivors,
Locking them away from society.
Out of my window, I see rescuers,
Gradually losing hope.
The city is stuck in slow motion,
Like a dream,
Only we won't wake up.

Clare Woods (13)
Sawston Village College

TRAPPED WITH A TWO SECOND MEMORY

They are trapped,
In a cage so small and cheap.
It's enough to make you weep
They were made from dust,
But what they want to do is bust.
Burst out of there
And live life to the fullest.

Note, they have this thought,
When they were bought
But with only a two second memory
It's hardly the best way to be!

They swim around a tub
In a mindless blub
Thinking what they have thought.

Patrick McCrae (13)
Sawston Village College

THE NIGHT

The stealthy sky filled up with night,
Just pure black darkness without no light.
The stars shine brightly with the moon,
The silver glow shines down with the gloom.
The crooked trees that arch their back,
Are very haunting when you walk the track.
Street lights are dim and hardly glows,
While the calm, gentle wind starts to blow.
The hours go by, and still no sight,
Of the sunrise in the eerie night.

Leon Cheng (14)
Sawston Village College

Union

How can we learn with no teacher,
How can we fly without wings,
How can we mend with no fingers,
And how with no voice, can we sing?

How can we run without legs,
How can there be 'Yes' without 'No'?
How can we dance with no music,
And can there be friend without foe?

The present locus of our being
Is dependent on fraternity,
We are all angels,
Born with one wing,
Hand in hand we fly.

Jasmine Phillips (14)
Sawston Village College

Star Light

Tiny little light bulbs lighting up the dark sky,
The little things 'out there' that people look at each night.
A dream world of infinite possibilities,
That light up the sky at night.

All the pictures you can make dotted around the sky,
Illuminating, flooding the sky with tiny bursts of energy!
I wonder what's up there now, for all I know
Could be anything!
The starlight won't last forever but where will it go?

Aron Murray (13)
Sawston Village College

My Head

In it there is a camera, waiting for me,
Hollywood, to make me a famous star.

In it there is a jungle with a long path
Leading to it, away from any life.

In it there is a knot, how do I untie it,
Which loop first?

Inside my head there is a fire,
Burning hot like my temper.

Inside my head there is a roundabout,
Which way do I turn?

In it there is a pair of scissors
To cut down my worries.

James Camp (12)
Sawston Village College

The Sun

I opened the window to get some fresh breeze,
When a blast of light was thrown at me,
I did not move and did not breathe,
As the shiny round object did not leave,
But when time passed, I dared to run,
And I went outside to see what was wrong . . .
And guess what it was . . .
The wonderful sun.

Serena Flack (13)
Sawston Village College

WHO IS THIS STRANGER?

Who is this stranger gazing back at me,
His eyes like darkened holes?
No happiness painted on his scrawny face.
His pride, stolen from better creatures.

Who is this stranger staring back at me,
His strength hidden within his tobacco pipe?
No expression shown but sadness.
Trapped within the fears of his trodden path of mystery.

Who is this stranger watching me,
Glancing over his shoulder at every sudden footstep?
Who shudders at every cry or grunt
A slug from his bottle
A short sign of ease within.

Who is this stranger gaping at me?
This stranger
Is no stranger
But me
The vermin of the streets.

Charlotte Judd (12)
Sawston Village College

REALITY

A crash, heard in the distance, but where?
The north tower, smoke creeps,
Like a prowler, crawling in the night.
Panic, all over; we're all thinking the same,
Who did it? Who's dead? Who'll take the blame?

I stumbled through the rubble,
Dust fell like snow, entangling in my hair,
I saw crying eyes, wishing wells,
Lives are taken, total despair.

Olivia Smith (13)
Sawston Village College

NIGHT SWEEPER

Night is like a black sheet
Spreading itself slowly
And lightly around the world.
Almost like a person
Flying through the sky.

Moonlight shining on the
Velvet sky.
Stars glistening high above
Then slowly the black dissolves
Turning into dawn
Once again.

Lucy Squire (13)
Sawston Village College

IN MY BED

When I'm tucked up in my bed at night,
I see through transparent curtains
And watch the moon pass by,
Bright sparkling stars glisten in the dark velvet sky,
I look back on the things that happened today,
And laugh and smile at the things my friends do and say.

Kelly Tombs (13)
Sawston Village College

THE NIGHTMARE

I can't go to school today - I don't feel well,
I lie to my mum, guiltily.
Her eyes meet mine and she knows I am fibbing,
And I am bundled into the car.

The five minute journey seems like five hours in ending
My mind is racing,
As I desperately try to decide
What my defence will be today.

I enter the school gates - the playground is normal -
People laughing, playing, talking, running,
I wish I could be so content
But I know that soon the nightmare will begin.

Around a corner - there they are
Standing in a large group, towering above me
The taunting, kicking and slapping start
'Oh look - here comes the baby elephant,' they laugh.

I pretend to ignore the names they call me,
But inside it hurts - like a dagger in my heart
As I try to gulp down
The lump in my throat.

At home I act as usual,
'How was your day luv?' 'Fine.'
I know it will happen again and again
I suffer in silence.

Lucinda Broad (13)
Sawston Village College

ON THE STREETS

I only just noticed him as I walked past,
His arms and legs like sticks,
Shrivelling up through lack of food.
His body leaned forward,
Alert as a meercat looking for danger.
His eyes not really tuned into this world,
But to a parallel universe.
Where he is rich and lives in a big house,
Not worrying where his next meal will come from,
Or where he will sleep that night.
Where he can take things for granted,
Like running water,
Or central heating.
Where he is respected and maybe even liked,
By other people.
Not being scowled upon,
Or made to feel
As if his only home is a dark corner,
With the rubbish and the rats.
I walk on by,
Keeping slightly away.
Then I make myself turn back,
And give him some money,
After all I can go home to my wife and my children,
But he's just there,
Alone on the streets.

Emily Brisley (12)
Sawston Village College

I Am:

A bright torch,
A source of light,
The night's light,
Craters surround me,
My baby stars following my every move,
A field of shining light,
God's lantern,
A lonely, quiet crater,
Earth's shadow,
The sun's brother,
The glitter of space,
Still and cold

What am I?

Answer: The moon

Robert MacKenzie (11)
Sawston Village College

September 11th 2001

A blanket covers the Earth
Silencing the world
Tragedy struck
Upon the Earth
People are shocked
At the horror that ruined
So many lives
Young, old or new
Lost in a movie scene
How can it be true?

Jessica Goody (14)
Sawston Village College

MY HEAD

In it there is water and ice
To refresh my mind

And there is a key
The key to life

And there is time
So I don't have to rush

A book anxiously waiting to be opened
A new world waiting to be found

A devil waiting to be awakened
An adventure waiting to jump out

A robot thinking my thoughts
And doing my homework!

A cheetah to take me away.
A wave wiping out my memory
And a cloud to take me high in the heavens.

A light bulb that flashes
Each time I have an idea or an answer to a question.

A fire growing each time I am angry

In it there is life with creatures
And thoughts and feelings as strong as diamonds.

Catarina Constância (12)
Sawston Village College

FOOTBALL? ... *IS IT ONLY JUST A GAME?*

It isn't the result of every game . . .
It's the result of every tackle,
Every decision by the referee.
It's the result of every x-ray from injuries,
And the result of every manager's half-time team talk.
It's the result of every offered contract for tens of thousands per week,
And there's also the result of every shot
That cost some people thousands of pounds (by betting).

Football, what do you mean 'It's only a game'?
People's lives depend on it. It's their job.
If it was, there wouldn't have to be any x-rays,
Or no harassing the man in black for a silly decision
Would there?
If it's only a game, why is it Britain's favourite sport?
How about rugby, tennis and even Monopoly!

Football, does anyone need to get injured?
Is it really necessary to spend £50 million on a signature?
No! . . . that's the answer.
If this sport is only a game why is there so much violence?
Even people dying.
Would pubs get packed while screening a golf competition?
Would the beer sales go up?
When people tell you it's only a game,
Did they take these facts into consideration?
I know my answer so I ask myself, is this necessary?

Is football really just a game?

No!

Jamie Elston (13)
Sawston Village College

IN MY HEAD

In my head there is a time traveller and an aeroplane.
The aeroplane will take me back where I'm from.
The traveller will take me back in time and back again
So I can fix all my mistakes and never have to worry again.

I can see peace and quiet, birds singing
And a beautiful, long, cold waterfall
With a warm sun reflecting on it to cool my anger down.

I can also hear soft classical music playing.
Stress, sorrow, worry and sadness will there be no more.
Not in my world there won't.

I see only smiles and laughter.
I will be cheered up and no word like 'sadness' will ever exist again.
Not in my world, not ever.
There will only be sweet voices of singing angels
And the sweet smell of roses.

My world is a fantasy world
With games and theme parks.
A world that once existed called Earth
But was destroyed by people.
In my head that world still exists, and will never end.
It will make me forget about everything I ever worried about.

The sun will always shine for there will be no darkness
And nothing evil but only peace and love.
Everything will be sweet and gone will be the bitter of the world.

More, more, more and even more.

Coba Vermaak (13)
Sawston Village College

THE HORSE

At Play

Fast as wind, thundering hooves, sleek
and agile with a noble head,
A flowing mane and whipping tail,
Nostrils flared, wild eyes, every sense is alive!

At Rest

Grazing calmly and relaxed,
each leg resting in turn.
Its eyes are dreamy
Its body covered in mud from rolling,
Every sense is at its best.

Samantha Rule (13)
Sawston Village College

WHEN THE LIGHTS GO OUT

When the lights go out I see creatures all around me
I see them hiding behind the doors
And I hear them in my chest of drawers
I hide under the covers and listen to the floor squeak
And now and then I dare to peek
To see if they have gone
Then I turn the light back on
And suddenly they all disappear,
Never again to reappear
Until the lights go out.

Craig Plater (13)
Sawston Village College

MY HEAD

Inside my head there is a ghost,
to make myself invisible,
this is the thing I wish most,
I don't like being seen.

Inside my head there is a mouth
chattering all day,
it tells jokes, it sings songs,
will it stop? No way!

Inside my head there is a spaceship,
to get away from here,
to fly with the clouds
and let all the aliens cheer.

Inside my head there is grass
as green as green can be
I play on it all day,
well all my friends and me.

Sarah Phillips (12)
Sawston Village College

A GODDESS?

Her eyes shine like stars at night,
Her beautiful hair is alike an angel,
Her looks are what everybody adores,
Boys drool over her stunning figure,
Her personality resembles Mother
Teresa,
I wonder and ponder,
Is she a goddess or is she human?

Nathaniel Nye (13)
Sawston Village College

WILL THEY COME BACK?

'Will they come back, Ma?'
I asked, waving off
My brother and Pa
As we stood in the street.

'I don't know pet, but we'll
Hope for the best.'
Something in her voice
Didn't sound at rest.

Is it the last time
I'll see them both?
I hope they'll be all right.

Later that month
We got a letter
Pa had been injured
But was getting better.

Is all we can do
Just sit and wait
Like the last puppy
In a litter of eight?

When will it end?
What can I do?
Just hope that one day
I'll see both of you?

What can I do?
Just sit and wait,
Waiting for you
To walk in
Through our gate?

Sinead Mathias (13)
Soham Village College

ONE DAY

I dream of the day when I will see him again
I read his letters, I pray for him.
I write him letters day and night
Hoping he will read them.
I hope one day he will see his son.

We will be waiting
For you to come back.
One day we will be
Together.

I wonder what he is doing.
Fighting? Sleeping? Writing? Dying?
I hope that one day
We will be
Together.

The first letter said he was wounded
The second said he was dead.
How can we be
Together
Now?

Years later, after the war,
I read his letters
I bring poppies to his grave
I hope that one day
We will be
Together
Forever.

Dieuwertje Laker (13)
Soham Village College

THE CARIBBEAN

Red, yellow, green and black,
The colours of the Caribbean,
Red of the steel bands,
Music played on old steel drums,
Dance away until morning comes.

Red, yellow, green and black,
The colours of the Caribbean,
The sea of custard, milky yellow,
People sunbathe to change colour,
Ball games are played
Until darkness covers
The wide expanse of glorious colours.

Red, yellow, green and black,
Colours of the Caribbean,
Green for the islands
Like peas in a pod,
Strung out over miles
From Havana in Cuba to
Port of Spain in Trinidad and Tobago
Discovered by Columbus in 1642.

Red, yellow, green and black,
Colours of the Caribbean,
Black for the soil
So fertile and warm
The rainfall is high
So tropical fruits grow
Banana, pineapple to export,
Coconuts too, all good for you.

Red, yellow, green and black,
Colours of the Caribbean,
A laid back lifestyle
No hurry or rush,
A poor existence,
No luxury goods to be found.

Christopher Reed (12)
Soham Village College

THAT HORRID FIELD OF DEATH

I run, run as fast as I can
Through that horrid field of death
To the barbed tangle of wire.
I find a way through
And see squadrons of men
Shooting at me.
I turn to see my men following me
And then feel a sharp pain
I fall and join the dead
In that horrid field of death.

As I look on to that field of death
Where I fought for England, my country
I remember the men I fought with
I remember my final charge at the enemy
As I went on to death
I remember how my men followed me.
I remember how I couldn't see
Through the gloom in front of me.
I remember wondering how many dead
Had crossed the line in front of me
On that horrid field of death.

Joshua Woodroffe ((13)
Soham Village College

Burning Light . . .

I know a place
Where scorpions scuttle
Under the burning light
Indestructible army shells
With stinging radar top.
Passing spiky flowers,
They dart in red dust under burning light.
Big heat swelling to a tremorous wave,
A centipede racing to a heatproof bunker.
Turtle trails dried up
Leading to deep, damp holes
Evaporating pool under the burning light.

Automatic springing frogs
Multicoloured in the mud
Burnt rubber carob pods
Twisting in the dust.

I know a place
Where autopilot eagles float and flop
Above the burning light.

Isaac McGinley (12)
Soham Village College

Show Me

Show me the Great War's triumph
Show me the things we gained
Show me the lives that were saved and treasured
That you did not die in vain.

Tell me what I know is wrong
Tell me it was worth the pain
Tell me it wasn't a waste of effort or of lives
That you did taste brief glory.

A broken heart is nothing.
Like Romeo and Juliet
As sweet and right as a heart can be
It's you my heart will never forget.

Show me the Great War's triumph
Show me the things we gained
Show me the lives that were saved and treasured
That you did not die in vain.

Rachele Guggiari (13)
Soham Village College

DAWN

Dawn appeared over the horizon
In a cascading blue gown
Singing her angelic song.

She smiles at the fluttering nightingale
Dancing on her shoulder
Gliding gracefully
On her enchanted unicorn
She travels down to earth
Dipping and rising
Flowers turning their heads
Hoping to catch a glimpse
Of the heavenly sight.

'Rise, don't stay in bed,'
She sings like a lullaby in my ear
Birds joining in her classical song
Riding on the unicorn.

Sea wakes and shimmers and glistens
And is dawn put to rest for another day.

Katie Rushforth (12)
Soham Village College

IN THE FIELD OF POPPIES

In the field of poppies
A kind, innocent soldier lay.
He'd done nothing to deserve this
His wish was to do his country proud.

He was only sixteen.

I saw him lying there
Still and quiet as if he were asleep
But when I tried to wake him
He wouldn't move.

At least he achieved his wish
He's done his country proud.
I remember his face
As pale and as white as chalk.

In the field of poppies
A kind, innocent soldier was
Laid to rest.

Kyle Mucha (13)
Soham Village College

UNDER FIRE

Everyone underground
Sitting like lemons
Listening to the shelling sound
Shrieking like harmless children.

All out on the firing line
We wait like prowling tigers
We listening to the shelling sound
To the shrieking of harmless children.

Enemy soldiers man their lines
Through the dust they yell
Someone shouted 'fire'
The shrieking went on all around
And like a horror film, we fell.

Sarah Paines (13)
Soham Village College

WATCHING THE RAIN

I wake to a cold shower
A miserable quietness drowning my house
Like a running tap
Filling up a bath
And through the speckled window of darkness
I see trees
Of the forest moaning
At the downpour
Flooding all the land
A groaning grey
That makes me want to sleep.

I wake to a cold shower
A miserable quietness drowning my house
Groans of cows
Gently stirring me to sleep
And sounds of music
Like the charm of splashing puddles
To this smell of porridge and jam

And this cold shower of night
Turns into the soft tongue
Of my dog.

Sarah Gillett (13)
Soham Village College

CARIBBEAN SECRETS - SENSE THE SUN

If I could see the orb of light I'd see,
Sapphire depths of aquatic bliss,
Exotic swimming ballerinas of the sea,
An array of the ocean's children, all in that ball.

The sphere ablaze in the azure silk holds images within.

If I could see the orb of light I'd see,
Foamy horses charging to shore,
Only to be dragged back to charge again,
Amber sands in all its glory, all in that ball.

The sphere ablaze in the azure silk holds images within.

If I could smell the orb of light I'd smell,
Bizarre spices of native origin,
A scent of nocturnal flowers,
Ocean's creatures ready for consumption, all in that ball.

The sphere ablaze in the azure silk holds scents within.

If I could hear the orb of light I'd hear,
Language of native people,
The busy music of the street,
The street's sound, all in that ball.

The sphere ablaze in the azure silk holds sounds within.

If I could feel the orb of light I'd feel,
Silky smoothness of pebbles on shores,
Rough texture of the coconut,
Tranquil breezes landing on my face, all in that ball.

The sphere ablaze in the azure silk holds textures within.

If I could taste the orb of light I'd taste,
Flavours of ocean spray, in the flowering breeze,
Vibrant relish of an island recipe,
Strange plants in unheard of meals, all in that ball.

The sphere ablaze in the azure silk holds flavours within.

Ryan Crockford (11)
Soham Village College

MORNING

The bright dazzling morning
Gliding noiselessly into the house
She gently stroked the cat
And sharply patted the dog.

She sang softly to the baby
And whispered quietly to the mother
She swept over the postman
And yelled loudly at the paperboy.

She tickled the mice
Asleep over the crackly floorboards
Then she crept to the garden.

She sparkled at the birds
In their fragile nest
She dazzled the flowers in their bed
Then left wet dew drops on the green grass

Day slowly began
As morning rode soundlessly down the street.

Craig Parnell (12)
Soham Village College

THE KEY TO THE DOOR

This is the key that opened the door
The door through time
To the first man
Who picked up a stone to shape another.

This is the key that opened the door
The door to the heavens
To the first gods
Who took the clay that made the Earth.

This is the key that opened the door
The door to the skies
Where stars are old worlds
Holding hidden peoples.

This is the key that opened the door
The door to the sea
Where the dolphin roams
Wondering what those lights are far, far above.

This is the key that opened the door
The door to the room
Where a lone figure sits
To write a poem
About the key that opened the door
In my head.

Natasha Pulley (12)
Soham Village College

IN THE MIDDLE OF NOWHERE

I turn off down the sandy track
And under the tunnel,
I crawl through the tiny, leafy hole in the hedge.

Bright sunshine beams through,
Soft breezes in the air,
Blue sky up above,
In the middle of nowhere.

Secretly twinkling lie streams and cobblestones,
Bridges made of long wooden sticks,
Willow trees in the middle of the stream,
I climb up the trees and lie on the branches
Watching the water flowing underneath me
As the leaves glide swiftly on.

I get up
And sit by the water's edge,
Skimming the pebbles
On the glittering surface of the stream
And watch the ripples shimmering in the sunlight.

I walk back through bulrushes
Under the trees, over the bridges,
Through the leafy hole in the hedge,
Under the tunnel, along the sandy track
And back home.

Amy-Louise Rankin (12)
Soham Village College

THE RIGHT ONE

I wish I was back in the sea
With waves towering over me
Watching and waiting for the right one
For soon it will come
Sweeping over the ocean.

When it does come
I feel it beneath me
Like an unseen moving force
Pushing me on, faster and faster.

I swoop and turn around everything in my path
I squeeze everything out of the wave

With no energy left it dies
I stall out
And wait for another

James Turner (12)
Soham Village College

ALL IN A DREAM

I run across no-man's-land
Past blackened stumps of trees
Past holes in the ground where bombs lie hidden
Ready to explode with a crying soldier's scream.
Why?
Is this all a dream?

I run fast and swift
A soldier appears out of the mist
I shoot, and again
But I miss as if no one was there.
Why?
Is this all a dream?

Like a cat trying to swim in the water
I try to run through no-man's-land.
Why?
If only
This was all a dream.

Jason Allen (13)
Soham Village College

FIELDS OF WAR

In the fields that lie so quiet
Like wind on a summer's day
Out we come to bring them gifts
To lay flowers for them by their graves
To weep and cry over days of war
That are now so far behind
In the fields that lie so quiet
Like wind on a summer's day.

There they rest in peace
So sombre, still and silent
Their families pray, wishing they were still here
For their fading memories are becoming unclear
For it is now so long
Since those days of war
And there they rest in peace
In those fields so sombre
So still
So silent
Like wind on a summer's day.

Meredith Thorpe (13)
Soham Village College

The Annual Trip

It starts the same every year
'Quick everyone, up or we'll be late!'
The car's all ready,
First stop is the gate
Put the card in, the gates open,
And the search is on to find the caravan.
Found it.
Now to get everything out of the car,
It's done and my first thought is, it's Sunday,
After tea we go to the club behind the caravans
We get our drinks
My sister, my brother and I play with the clown
We join in the competitions
Then we get our badge and certificate.

The next day we go to the beach
Where the tractor got stuck the other year
After that it's the swimming pool
We play with the twins in the big pool
Mum and Dad get a cup of tea
While William plays in the small pool with a slide.

The week has flown by
So we have a quick stop in Mundesley
Before finally going home.

Charlotte Woodbridge (15)
Soham Village College

ARIZONA

So hot and dry with a cool breeze,
But come July monsoon season will change routine,
About a foot of rain and a big dust wall
Will soon be gone as soon come.
The sun rises from the canyon
So great with rivers and caves throughout,
Coyotes run free, as lizards crawl,
As snakes wander through cactus plains,
Beetles sprint across the red hot sands.
A tribe will be moving as since native times
Seeking to be free.
The tumble weeds big and bushy,
Huge Jack rabbits run freely by
Like wind upon water
But watch for the bird so fast and small
We all know as the roadrunner.

Take a walk down the street, no need for shoes
Take a trip to the 7-11 where drinks are best
Driving by palm trees lining the roads
Kids will be in swimming pools
Don't forget cowboys and cattle
The western towns buried in deep ravines.

What you'll find is fun and mystery
In the grand state of Arizona.

Frankie Houck (13)
Soham Village College

I Miss My Mum

Dear mother I sit and wonder why,
I sit and wonder
Ponder for all this time
Sometimes at night I cry
At night I walk far from war as I can
The gun fire so bright
It seems like day
Writing just to reach you

No worries for me I am fine
Although there is plenty of time for us
I fear the worse is yet to come
The day for this war is not yet done
All the time new men recruited
To fight to die no sense at all

Forever I may think of home
To fall in your arms
Safe from harm
You always know just what to say

Beth Fuller (13)
Soham Village College

If I Could Capture

If I could capture
A butterfly
It would be
The diamond of my eye
It would scare away the wet, wet days
And cheer me up
(It has its ways)
It would flutter about
Like a petal in the breeze.

But then comes the day it has to leave
I'd let it go
I'm not that cruel you know
It would be my childhood
Flying away
Because here comes the chains of adulthood
Come to bind me down.

Harriet Wright (13)
Soham Village College

WAITING

There she sat, waiting, waiting,
Waiting for her husband,
She was waiting like a hawk
Waiting for a mouse,
One sound, one tiny sound,
She would be up to see if it was him.

There she sat waiting, waiting,
Waiting for her husband,
She sat there waiting like she was
Waiting for a cake to rise,
The letters have stopped,
She used to get two a week.

There she sat waiting, waiting,
Waiting for her husband,
He went away a year ago,
He hasn't been back since.
I don't think he is coming back,
Not today, not tomorrow, not ever.

Charlotte Avison (13)
Soham Village College

BLACKPOOL

The train pulls up at the station
And comes to a final halt
We step into a taxi and take the familiar journey
To my grandparents' house.

The smell of dinner cooking
Is clear when we enter
It feels more like a second home.

Long walks by the sea
Look down at the donkeys on the beach
The tower in the distance
Arcades along the seafront.

In October the place is lit up
The illuminations draw in the tourists.

On the way home we pick up chips,
A tradition for everyone
When it comes to go home everyone is sad,
'But don't worry,' we say,
'We'll be back again soon.'

Kimberley Ashwell (14)
Soham Village College

THE FOREST

Trees make a canopy that cover the sky
We're watching the birds as they fly.

The creek bubbles and spits
It turns into a river
Washing away everything it hits.

The mountainside where the forest is,
Is covered in boulders
They're smothered in moss,
Every nook and cranny.

Leaves fall to the ground
Twisting round and round.

Lucy Gray (13)
Soham Village College

QUIETLY

Day came in
As an angel
With the mist and dew following behind.
She quietly flew down
A quiet urban street.
With her sparkly, small wand
She drew a pale yellow object
Away from all the fog and cloud.
She saw a quiet, little baby
And gently touched it.

She flew by gently.
The mist and dew flew by her.

From house to house
Street to street
She stroked them softly
She gracefully prods the old, drooping tree
With a starling in it.

A slash of blue
Crept around the corner.

Amanda Pettit (12)
Soham Village College

FIREWORKS

One year we went to Geneva,
We travelled for a long time.

One night we went to a city,
And down to the river.
We waited by the river,
In the dark, on a warm night.

Then suddenly a gold streak of fire,
Exploded in the air
Showering gold sparks everywhere,
The fireworks had started.
The boats on the river,
Decorated as animals
Letting off colours of fire into the sky,
Then a big bang
And they scatter into the river
On the mountains in the distance,
More fireworks are let off.

Then it stops,
And people go home.

We left the river,
We left the city,
We left that night behind.

Helena Evans (12)
Soham Village College

MOVING WORLD

Spinning, spinning,
The whole world is spinning
Jungle to ocean
City to town.

Growing, growing,
The whole world is growing
Cottage to 'scraper
Acorn to oak

Travelling, travelling,
The whole world is travelling
US to UK
North to the south

Living, living,
The whole world is living
Insect to elephant
Human to dog

Breathing, breathing,
The whole world is breathing
Plants and animals
Village, city and town

Spinning, spinning,
The whole world is spinning
Forever weaving
Down life's crooked path.

Shona Daly (12)
Soham Village College

The Faces Of The Enemy

A yawning soldier rested on the fire-step
In the ferocious glare of the beaming sun.
Bullets screamed by.
'Come on!' yelled a panicking commander
The quivering soldier sighed.

We clambered through squelching mud
Rifles at the ready
We held our positions
Battle sounds pierced the haze
Fire!

Our whistling bullets sang like a blackbird's morning call
One by one soldiers were being picked off
As they valiantly climbed over the barbed wire.
Our machine guns spat angrily.

Could this be the face of the enemy?

Oliver Williams (13)
Soham Village College

Trickle Of The Water

Trickle of the water, brightness of the sun,
The juiciness of the mangoes, aren't I the lucky one?
The blueness of the sea and the blueness of the sky
These are the sorts of things I see with my two eyes.

The music of the drums make the trees sway
I hear the music every night and hear it every day.

Trickle of the water, the brightness of the sun,
The juiciness of the mangoes, aren't I the lucky one?
The milk in a coconut and the whiteness of the sand
How lovely it feels as it runs right through
The softness of my hand.

Trickle of the water, the brightness of the sun,
The juiciness of the mangoes, aren't I the lucky one?

Thomas Seljamae (12)
Soham Village College

DAYBREAK

Day arrived on a white stallion
With two friends singing peacefully
They woke up mothers and babies.
Lush trees, bright flowers, colourful birds,
All woke up at the sound of their peaceful song

Day glistened and sparkled like nothing before.
Lovebirds sun as day
And two friends turned the dark corner.

Day began to rise, tulips opened,
Trees swung in the cool breeze.
They woke up lazy sweepers, postmen, milkmen
That went to their early morning round.

The two friends disappeared
As day flew up to the bright soft blue sky.

Sarah Bayes (12)
Soham Village College

EXOTIC PLACES

I love exotic places,
The smell of the sun and the sea,
The clear blue water,
The hot, burning sand
Covering my feet
The people's chatter,
The laughter, the music,
The warm breeze,
The lush green palm leaves,
The juicy fruits
All different in their own special way,
The children playing
The friendly people on the street,
Different things to drink and eat,
This is where I'd like to be,
I love exotic places.

Tori Atkinson (12)
Soham Village College

THE ROAD

The road stretches on endlessly
The sight sores my eyes
The dust catches in my throat
The heat sends sweat trickling down my back
I think of home
Why did I do this?
What did I choose?
To travel, to journey, to discover.

The speed of the road
The noise of the road
Is what I want
Is what I dream
The tension of hope
The light of discovery
Teases me
And finds me.

Caroline Watson (12)
Soham Village College

THAT LITTLE BLUE CHALET

Oh how I long for that feeling of warmth
As I opened the door
The rocking chair sitting there in the corner
The sound of the creaking bunk beds
The calm peaceful mornings
The little pool to swim in
The arcades and Bingo to play
The restaurant and chip shop
We visited every day.
To walk to the empty beach
Gentle waves washing my hand
The memories of our holiday
The castles made of sand

Oh how I long for
That little blue chalet.

Emma Badcock (14)
Soham Village College

WASTE OF LIFE

Sitting, waiting, shaking,
Too nervous to talk
Listening to the shells
Waiting for the signal
To go over the top.

There it is.
Bullets fly like a flock of geese.

Does anyone care for the lives that are lost
For the boys tricked into becoming
A bunch of corpses
Like half dead plants
Littering the ground?

Rachel Peachey (13)
Soham Village College

CARIBBEAN BEACH

A yellow ball hanging in the sky
Grains of gold, setting on the ground,
A bright blue ocean sparkling like diamonds.

Cubes of spices filling the air with sweet smell
The crunch of grinding coffee.

The sound of the steel filling the silence.

Hitting a six,
Hitting it high
Into the yellow ball
Hanging in the sky.

Alex Fogg (12)
Soham Village College

GREEN EYES OF ENVY

The face of death,
Ghostly and green.
The colour seeping out
Into the counterpane.

Soon to depart
The lush green Earth,
Its leafy bows
And patchwork fields.

Small green blades
Alive with caterpillars,
Clicking grasshoppers
And croaking frogs.

Green the unripe,
Heading for a future.
Mouldy am I
Yet still am I green.

Final look on this world,
I wish I could stay.
Green twigs will bend
But I am soon to break.

Young men of this world
Are fresh and green,
So upon them I look
With green eyes of envy.

David Aylmer (13)
The Leys School

Red

Red
The colour
Of a boxer's glove.
Anger, hatred,
Love.
A cricket ball,
A toucan's beak,
A post box
Waiting on the street.
Red
The cavern
Of a lion's jaw.
Onlookers engrossed,
Gazing in awe.
Beneath the waves,
Red coral lies,
Modest to all
But prying eyes.

Red
The glow
Of a neon sign.
Peppers, chillies,
Wine.
A crusader's cross,
A laser beam.
The red book
Of Mao's strict regime.
Red
The colour
Of bankruptcy,
Culprits engulfed
By poverty.

Red lava devours
All it sees,
And casts in stone
For eternity.

Madeleine Williams (13)
The Leys School

IMAGES OF GREEN

Green as the finch
with feathers so bright.
Green as the house
which lets in the light.
Green as the fingers
of a gardener so rare.
Green as the child
so easy to scare.
Green as the fly
never to stop.
Green as the smell
of a good summer crop.
Green as the blooming of
young buds
in May.
Green as the grass
so tender to lay.
Green is the life,
which given a chance,
can open the doors to
laughter and dance.

Adam Arnot Drummond (14)
The Leys School

RED

Red is love and an air of passion
Red is the colour of rivals clashing.
Fox's tails are sometimes red,
And the rose of memorial, to honour the dead.
Red is the blood,
Of the wound from a spear,
And the colour of sunset,
As evening draws near.
Heat of a fire
And gnarled hands of the old
The tiny, red noses
Of kids out in the cold.
Mars is red
As a star of the night
And the glow from a boat
With a port side light.
The embers of flames,
That will glow forever,
And the colour of
Fresh phoenix feathers.
Red is the colour
Of strawberries ripe.
And is half of the lines
On the stars and the stripes.
A cockerel's crest,
As it stands in the sand
Albino eyes
And Coca-Cola cans.

Chris Colgate (13)
The Leys School

RED

Red is the sun,
Gazing down like an angry eye,
Burning pale cheeks red.
Red is love,
And a cherry of blood,
Gushing out of a cut finger.
Red is a diminutive ladybird,
crawling up my arm,
Red is anger,
Red is hell,
Red is rubies,
Set into a priceless ring,
Red is a rose,
Blossoming in the spring,
Making the countryside glimmer,
With warmth.
Red is tomatoes,
Red is lush lips,
Covered in strawberry juice.
Red is a post box
And the stamps on letters to,
Just waiting to be posted to you.
Red in a rainbow arching through the sky,
Its fellow colours following closely by.
Red-hot peppers burn your tongue.
Red-hot pokers,
Stand proud.

Kate O'Brien
The Leys School

RED SKY

Red sky at night, shepherd's delight,
Strawberries dipped in cream the way I like,
Teachers are marking in red of course,
Embarrassment comes for a racing horse,
Blood-stained sails coming back from war,
Awaiting are those loved-ones, from whom they were torn,
Caught red-handed as they wield their swords,
Safe are those in the House of Lords,
Rose-red bodies line the sunkissed beach,
A tired out man eats a tomato quiche,
Smells of autumn as flames leap higher,
Leaves writhe in the hell fire,
Anger burns with America's mourning,
Red sky in the morning, shepherd's warning.

Laura Taylor (13)
The Leys School

RED

The soldier, his heart of flames,
Burning with anger,
Letting out rage,
Striding with braveness,
Bodies left for days,
Leaving the battlefield empty of love,
An angry fire burning,
Poppies left there stained in blood.

Carla Swift (12)
The Netherhall School

Scorpio Sonnet

Scorpio's a water sign, water's your love.
Sports like swimming, diving, are just fun.
You're clever, you're funny, you're bossy too.
Your needs are love, attention, affection
You were born between the twenty-third of October
To the twenty-second of November.
Your perfect mums's a Pisces
Or maybe a Scorpio. Your fab dad's a Taurus
Or maybe a Capricorn.
Your best brother is a Capricorn and
Sister's a Sagittarius.
Your best teacher's a Capricorn,
You work with well
Scorpio's a water sign, water's your love.
Sports like swimming, diving are just fun.

Fizza Mirza (12)
The Netherhall School

Fire Ball

Fast flaming fireball
Moving through space
Colour of red, orange
The flames are very hot

The fireball is so hot like the sun
Bits of it come off the sun
And die out
In the atmosphere

The fire spot sparks
Like a rocket on Burns Night.

Lee Fowle (14)
The Netherhall School

VAMPIRE!

He sleeps, upside down.
His cape falls limply over his shoulders
I can hear him breathing, in and out, it's slow and death-like.
His profile is grey like the rain clouds.
His face is sharp like a knife.
He has two bat-like wings falling over his knees, they stay there
Like statues, not moving an inch.
I breathe in deep, the air is old and stale, it makes me feel sick.
I hold my hand over my mouth, my heart is hammering on my chest,
Trying to push itself out.
It's dark and damp, there is no sound at all.
Until he twitches.
His bat wings unfold and his grey face moves.
Then his black eyes flick open. He stares at me.
His eyes are like icicles, except not blue, they are black and powerful.
I freeze to the spot unable to move. He does not speak,
He just stares thoughtfully at me.
He opens his mouth and his teeth fall out onto his bottom lip.
They are razor sharp,
Their yellow stains cover almost all the white of his fangs.
A drop of saliva on the left hand side of the tooth
Slides down his lip and onto his chin.
I am so close I can smell that saliva,
It smells like blood,
It wants blood . . .
And then he smiles a cheeky smile. That vampire.

Leanne Haden (15)
The Netherhall School

A Fiery Poem

Volcanoes erupting are like a kettle boiling.
The molten rock is like a long trail of flaming petrol.
The lava is like a fiery snake.
That is eating everything in its path.
The sun is like a huge, fiery clock
It uses light to tell the time -
The sun is a huge light bulb
In the middle of the solar system.

A volcano is a very dangerous bomb
Getting ready to blow.
The tension keeps building
Higher and higher like a multi-storey car park.
Eventually it goes off
With a huge explosion
And spreading fire and lava everywhere
The war has begun.

Marc Brown
The Netherhall School

Wind!

Whistling along humming as she strolls away
Reaching out to feel the crisp green leaves
They rustle
She sweeps them up, they fly
A gentle lamb by day,
A fierce fox by night.
Howling through the darkness
Giving you a chill
She sails away!

Charlotte Okten
The Netherhall School

THE SEA AND THE MOON

The sea
She is blue
The moon glistens on her
The moon pale and white
He loves to shine upon the water, her feminine liquidity
They both go together so well
He loves her so
She is in love
But they are not meant to be
Because he is the moon and she is the sea
So all they can do is . . .
Glance at each other a million miles apart
The sea and the moon.

Bilesh Ladva (12)
The Netherhall School

THE POWER OF LOVE

Her house is high up on cloud nine
She is as pretty as a picture
With hair like a golden waterfall
With her red clothing she roams the street
Her voice is soothing and can mend a broken heart
Her job she loves as she gets to spread romance through the world
She secretly works day and night
The most powerful woman in the world.

Her name is
    Love!

Samantha Pearson (12)
The Netherhall School

THE TRAGEDY OF TITANIC

T errifying Titanic as it sank tragically.
I mmobile iceberg standing in the way of the ship.
T errible tragedy when the ship sank and al the people died.
A busive atmosphere as passengers push and shove
   trying to get on a lifeboat.
N eglected nervous people jumping overboard.
I cy ill people drowning in the sea.
C rying crowds in the wild water.

Amy McKechnie (11)
The Netherhall School

AUTUMN

A smouldering sunset
U p above the fiery trees
T he cry of a kestrel
U nderneath the clouds
M illions of crimson leaves carpet the ground
N ight-time falls, silently.

Verity Shelbourne (12)
The Netherhall School

THE DANCING FIRE

Fire is like a cheetah -
It can move really fast and it is yellow/orange
Fire is like a runner moving and going anywhere it wants
Fire is a teenager it dances all night long.

Hitanshu Barot (13)
The Netherhall School

FIRE

The fire is a snake,
Flames polluting the air,
Slithering, hissing,
Burning up inside,
A poisonous cobra,
Polluting the air,
The shape is the flames,
Spitting sparks like venom,
Hissing, polluting, hissing,
Can be hidden and suddenly spring out!
Fast, furious, hot!
Like a rattlesnake,
Rattle, rattle
The fire is a snake.

Rachel Prat (13)
The Netherhall School

AQUARIUS!

A fish swimming through the sea,
Q uiet as quiet as can be,
U nder the water down we go,
A mong the coral all does flow,
R ainbow coloured fish around,
I n the mind is sea to sound,
U nder the world down we go,
S inking deeper might we so.

Andrea-Claire Fordham
The Netherhall School

I'M AN AQUARIUS

I'm an Aquarius I love water
A water bearer by star, swimmer by nature,
I hold a jug pouring water
In the dark skies of January
And frosty nights of February, so cold.
As I walk in my costume and dive, dive
Into the lovely water so soft, smooth
I swim strongly, elegantly to the end,
Twenty five metres fast stretching out.
My stars shine brightly in the beautiful sky,
No clouds all stars just continuous flowing
For eternity for no end.
I'm an Aquarius, I love water
Water bearer by star, I love water.

Amy Cook (12)
The Netherhall School

THIS IS THE KEY TO THE WORLD

This is the key to the world
In the world there is a country
In the country there is a city
In the city there is a town
In the town there is a village
In the village there is a road
Down the road there is a house
In the house there is a girl sleeping
In the girl's sleep there is a dream
In the girl's dream there is love.

Love is the key to this world.

Jade Gatt (13)
The Netherhall School

THE SEA

The sea is a lioness and a cub
Calming, relaxing, gentle
A friendly creature
Caring in its own way
Looking into each other's eyes
Deep, unknowing

The sea is a lion
Dangerous, harmful, scary
A horrible creature
Roaring, crashing, nightmare
Glaring into your eyes
Deep, unknowing

The sea is a killer lion
Frightening, shaky, ready to kill
A murderous creature
Not thinking, angry, over in a blink
Piercing your eyes
Deep, unknowing . . .

Sarah Norman (12)
The Netherhall School

RED SNOW

The chickens are alive
In the cold, still air
With the darkness deepening
What could harm them?

And then, through the soft, white snow
A sly body appeared
With a pointed nose and bushy tail
It slithered under the wire fence

In the fear and confusion
A chicken is gone
The snow is red
But a stomach is filled.

Sarah Baron (12)
The Netherhall School

ATTACK

The planes glide overhead.
A crash,
A smash,
A bash,
Metal on metal,
Then mayhem.

The hours roll past,
The prospects grim,
Too late,
Too long,
They'll never be back.

The search goes on,
The days are one.
Disappear.
No hope.
The light of life dwindles.

What next?
Rebuild,
Recession,
Rebel,
Or just Respect!

Alistair Cray (15)
The Netherhall School

SUNKEN SHIP

Her majestic maiden voyage,
Delightful departure.
Titanic's dramatic decks were full of cramped cabins
And crowded corridors.

Sudden shudder.
The courageous captain calmed down the petrified passengers.
The rushing water ruined the restaurant and
Flooded the furniture.

The crushing walls of wild water spread.
Slowly sinking, deeper darker.
Sad sunken ship.

Helen Proffitt (12)
The Netherhall School

THE TRAGEDY OF TITANIC

Anchor away we set off today as she left Southampton
The crowds of people who were standing and cheering
Were to be so many tears.
As she glimpsed in the sun there was so much fun
But was it to be later?
One day had passed we were going quite fast
And swishing through the water.
In a matter of days she sprung a leak with a great, big crash.
The tears of laughter were about to be sorrow
As people were jumping from a height
Now she is sinking, she's about to be history
Which is something we will never forget.

Oliver Oakman (11)
The Netherhall School

THE TRAGIC SCENE OF THE TITANIC!

There was a beautiful boat called Titanic,
But something happened, it was dramatic,
Titanic was hit by an iceberg so high,
Why, why, oh why.
The corridors were crowded, and crying appeared.
The passengers were playing with no regrets,
Some people had come from the bath, soaking wet!
Launching ladies swaying in and out, holding their children without
                                                                                   no doubt.
Gelling gentlemen getting around, jumping off the sides,
Landing into the roaring tides.
Splitting in half Titanic sank,
Into the ocean she did go.
A lot of people will and a lot of people won't
Why did the Titanic sink?
Titanic was beautiful and was such a glory.
But now we have come to the end of this tragic story!

Charley Atherton (11)
The Netherhall School

THE DEATH OF THE TITANIC

The day began much the same
Who knew some friends we would never see again?
We shared the horror but some wouldn't see tomorrow.
The ship was struck deep in her heart.
Her insides torn apart.
Slowly she sank down - deep, deep
To her long, dark sleep.

Luke Latty (11)
The Netherhall School

The Anutaur (A Mythical Beast)

The anutaur wakes from its sleep,
Roaring, biting, stamping,
His teeth are curved swords,
His red tongue has the stench of blood,
The constant sadness of his heart,
Showing on his face in the form of fury and frustration,
His head is furry, almost like a coniferous forest.
His horns are black, as black as darkness
The anutaur's eyes are yellow,
They have slits for pupils, very much like a cat.
His arms are strong and muscular,
One has a metallic hand
With claws of steel,
The other one had a hoof.
His feet smelt of rot,
They had serrated claws,
Which were so sharp,
They could cut through anything,
Loneliness walks with him.

Ali Hammad (12)
The Netherhall School

The Sinking Ship

A lovely launch turned into a terrible terror.
The sinking ship full of crowded corridors and paranoid passengers
Slowly started to get lower into the water
As the nasty night went on the awful atmosphere got worse
The courageous captain tried to calm down paranoid passengers.

Rachel Philpott (11)
The Netherhall School

A Sonnet

I feel the need to be with you always,
I know the need to be with you is true,
And it's real when I say I count the days,
Until I can quietly lay with you.
We watch the shining sun and the high moon,
And the days run by as quick as they may,
But the nights without you come far too soon,
As I think of things I forgot to say.

I do not cry because I never could,
While my thoughts can dream quite so easily.
I know in my heart that I really should
Ask why I love you more than you for me.

What a strange feeling it is to feel this,
That I'd go to hell, just for one soft kiss.

Becky White (17)
The Netherhall School

The Titanic

It started off as a lovely sight,
But no one knew it would end up as a fright.
People crying
People dying
People fleeing for their lives
But that wasn't easy.
People couldn't believe their eyes as it was such a sight.
But this was such a fright.

Yaa Acheampong (11)
The Netherhall School

Thirteen Ways Of Looking At A Seat

I

The boy sits on his mother's lap
Two seats now taken

II

The chair rocks
An old lady rests

III

The suspect awaits; nervous
Empty spaces ready for the jury.

IV

Twenty people share the chair
Strangers
Twenty appointments before lunch.

V

The bench is free
Snow is falling fast;
Changing the face of its surroundings.

VI

Quiet;
Beneath the canopy, upon a fallen tree,
Sits a pondering soul.

VII

The car is empty,
Yet each place is taken.

VII

Another patient
Slowly moves into position
Tension.
Blurry eyed, waking slowly
Discomfort
Job complete.

IX

Small child's adventure
Sat between the bars,
Legs swinging
Head of the shopping

X

Naked sofa
Undressed image.

XI

Winter
The tall armchair placed in front of the fire
Warm, cosy -
Outside, ice.

XII

The lifeless man takes his seat,
This time he is the victim.
'Electricity shall now be passed through
Your body until you are dead.'
His sentence is served.

XIII

This seat may be binding,
For some, a lifelong bond.
Your independence, motivation,
Companion, your life.
All this run on wheels.

Catherine Darler (16)
The Netherhall School

BLACK AND WHITE

Black like the night
Bathing in the darkness
Blocking out the colours
Hiding them from view.

Black like outer space
Miles and miles of nothing
Stars appearing as holes
In the black, velvet cover.

White like paper
Waiting to be changed
Splotches of colour
Breaking the peace.

White like snow
Nothing, but whiteness
Wherever you look
And now, hoping for something else.

Oliver Francis (12)
The Netherhall School

TITAN TITANIC

Terrifying time
Incredible icebergs
Titan Titanic
Amazing atmosphere
Nervous night
Icy insurance
Courageous captain.

Hayley Burch (11)
The Netherhall School

RIDDLE

My parents are growing in a rainforest
My brothers are whose mistakes I pick up
I hope to be placed in a pencil case
With the rest of my family but
I'll probably just be worn away.

Answer: I am a rubber!

Liam Williamson (13)
The Netherhall School

MOON!

My moon
I love you so
You shine sweetly at me
You come to me on lonely nights
My love!

Lisa Randall (12)
The Netherhall School

TITANIC, THE SINKING SHIP

What a dramatic departure
Passengers being posh
Ready to go on the spectacular ship.
Courageous captain to cross
The oversized ocean.

Crowded corridors with
Comfortable cabins and a
Succeeding service.

A none forgettable night with a
Lovely luxury and an
Original orchestra.
What an amazing atmosphere!

Who knows what will happen?

A horrible thing just happened
Titanic hit the irresistible iceberg.
Those posh passengers became
Poor passengers.

The atmosphere became a sinister scene!

Flore Elisabeth Suter (11)
The Netherhall School

AWAKENING STORM

He awakes,
So angry,
His voice thunders,
Waking children.

His eyes flash,
So blindingly bright,
Making a zigzag shape,
In the ever darkening sky.

He cries,
So suddenly,
Tears splashing onto the ground,
Pools of water.

He blows,
So strongly,
Whistling through the sky,
And then he sleeps once more.

Alice Miller (12)
The Netherhall School

FIRE

The fire
The fire danced through the air
Bringing joy to its surrounders
The fire it's a magician
It pops up in a puff of smoke
Seducing people with its hypnotic charm
It writhes in and out of the air
It spits out its lethal, glowing embers
A mysterious yet beautiful object
But if you don't treat it right
It billows out smoke
Suffocating anyone who dares describe
As if it was stating that the fire was now in control
It grows and grows
Invading more and more space
Taking more and more victims
Becoming greedier and greedier
No longer a form of happiness
But now a form of hatred.

Jonathan Lander (12)
The Netherhall School

THE TITANIC TRAGEDY

Tremendous Titanic sets off
In the ship there are crowded corridors
The controlling captain looks happy,
And soon after there's a chaotic crash.
Now there are petrified passengers.
It looks like a terrible tragedy,
Causing the superb ship to sink.

Nesha Patel (11)
The Netherhall School

HEDGEHOG

What is a hedgehog?
Its body is like a pin cushion
Its nose is like a chocolate button.
Its face is as pointed as an ice cream cone
Its legs are like sewing pins.
Their feet are as sharp as an owl's eye
And it woodles through the night
Or it will turn into a ball if it has a fright.

Jodie Tucker (12)
The Netherhall School

THE FIRE IS A CAT!

The fire is a cat,
The flames purr the air,
The warmth is the cat
Cuddled up on the chair.

The colour of the sparks,
Is the colour of the hair.
It glows so bright,
It makes you stop and stare.

Charlotte Taylor (12)
The Netherhall School

POSEIDON

Nurtured down within the deep
Fathoms down in my sleep
Then in haste about my head
Sea creatures swimming full of dread

For thunder came across the waves
Its wake upon the water slayed
Fire and smoke, iron and steam
Its hulk of metal with silvered gleam

Filthy folk came from the lands
To pollute my world by their hands
With anger welling deep within
I took the ice and pierced its skin

My watery hands grasped the ship
And I took it deep within my grip
Their worthless souls cried to be free
But for eternity they'll dwell with me

I felt the hole within the beast
Now its smoky heart had ceased
Its conquered name upon its head
Titanic's glory now was dead

Denice Nowlan (12)
The Netherhall School

FIRE

A young hare leaping and dancing
The flames are like a firefly illuminating the air
He seems to laugh as he sends a shower of sparks from the heart
And smiles with glee as the logs settle
He eats away at the surrounding dark throughout the night
He makes sure everyone is warm and comfortable, then he begins
He tells everyone a story that will send them to sleep
As the sun rises he gets tired
And silently gets smaller and smaller
Until he is nothing but an orange glow
But his cheery face will return to laugh another day.

Sarah Holmes (12)
The Netherhall School

THE TRAGEDY OF TITANIC

We set off from the dock
And I'll assure you that no one would mock
The great power and grace of Titanic
And what was to happen to it *so* dramatic
The engines started 1, 2, 3
Coal was shovelled not easily
One night it hit an iceberg, rip, slice, tear
It was hard to believe and bear
That we would die simply
It may sound gruesome believe me!
The engines stopped 1, 2, 3
Coal was not shovelled, you see?

Andrew Flynn (12)
The Netherhall School

FIRE

Fire is a snake
Its dark, blood-red, slitted eyes
And it's forked-like tongue
Which differs from one hell to another
The snake
Has patterns of cold flames
On its scaly skin.

Fire is a witch's black cat
With eyes of curved swords
The cat spits flaming hot lava at anyone
Who's in its way.

Fire is the Devil
He holds a blood-red trident
And has a long, flick whip for his tail

Fire is a three-headed dog
Barking, boiling water
As if it was a blazing sun
When he feels like it.

Fire is hate.

Henry Stockley (12)
The Netherhall School

SNAIL CINQUAIN

Slow snail
Curly wurly
As it moves turning round
And round squashing underneath ne'er
    Stopping!

Marianna Murray (13)
The Netherhall School

PURPLE

An angry bruise screaming with pain.
The wacky streaks of a hippy's hair.
A spark from a magician's wand.
The bright but dark lights of a disco.
A magical mystical object peeping.
Through a cloud of mist.

Rachel Story (12)
The Netherhall School

THE ROAD TO CHINA

Tomorrow I'm going to China
Everything will be so different to me.
I'm used to life on a liner
For the first time in my life, I shall say
Farewell to the sea.

Oh how I do not want to leave!
The open ocean that I love.
The fresh breeze blowing to my face
And the dolphins that I love to chase
But I must do as they say, at dawn I go away.

Dawn is breaking. I am shaking
My life is in shreds now.
They are calling me, I must go
I wonder if the sea will ever forgive me.
If I leave, I will never see you again, farewell!

Veronica Andersson (12)
The Perse School For Girls

VAMPIRE

Raven-black eyes stare out at me, dark and foreboding.
A ghostly white face looks at me, hungrily.
A skeletal figure emerges out of the darkness,
Walking slowly, like a tiger stalking its prey.
Fear grips my heart in a hold it won't let go of,
Piercing into my very soul and being.
Dark hair lies on her shoulders,
Pointed teeth glinting in the moonlight.
I turn to run, but as I do so, she speaks.
'No.'
Just one word, that's all.
That's all it took for me to be frozen to the spot.
She creeps up behind me and puts her arm around my neck.
I can feel her cold breath on my neck,
I can smell her bloodlust, her rage.
I can see in her eyes she wants me dead.
I can hear an owl hooting in a tree somewhere.
I can taste the freedom in the air.
So near, yet beyond my reach.
I am beyond all help now.
Nothing can save me now.
I will die all alone.
A lonely and forgotten person
Hidden in the mists of time.
Her face is getting lower and lower towards my neck.
Sweat is running down my cheek.
Death is so near . . .
Her teeth sink into my neck.
All I can feel is immense pain.
Then I feel no more.

Rachel Armitage (11)
The Perse School For Girls

THE WORLD AT WAR

I was lying under six blankets,
But I was still cold.
The weather reflected my feelings perfectly,
Cold, Grey and damp.
The world had been at war for seven years.
Seven whole years without a single thing to celebrate.
Nothing seemed like it was worth living for.
So I ran my hand under my pillow.
I felt the cold surface of the knife,
The knife I had slept with for defence.
I drew it out and pressed point to my heart.
I took one long last look around the room.
Then pressed hard.
It was all . . .

   . . . Gone.

Eleanor Westgarth-Flynn (12)
The Perse School For Girls

A SILVER STITCH

Why does it have to unravel now?
Your silver stitch, inside you, is being picked at,
It's had too many rows.
You feel like you don't belong
Anywhere.

It used to shine in the moonlight,
It used to be the one who's right,
And now it doesn't, not anymore,
You might as well walk out of the door.

People tell it 'You interfere.'
People act strange when you are near.
Why does it have to unravel
Here and now?

Victoria Ball (11)
The Perse School For Girls

THE ABBEY

Crumbling ruins lie in peace
Beside the sparkling, winding river,
Birds sing sweetly in the trees
Around this pleasant, tranquil place.

Once this was an abbey grand
Where the black-robed canons dwelt,
Riding out across the land
To teach God's word to one and all.

Now what is left of that great strewn?
A doorway here, a jarred wall there,
Stone blocks strewn across the ground,
Memories long forgotten.

Only in the little church
Still stand the pillars vast and tall,
Intricate patterns laid in stone
Hundreds of years ago.

Susanna Bridge (11)
The Perse School For Girls

BEGINNING

In the beginning, there was nothing.
A black canvas of eternity.
She didn't know how she came to be, or when
But with her existence came energy.
Enraptured, she clapped, and fragments
Of joy broke away, to shine vivaciously,
Against the deep velvet of the universe.
Her radiant face embellished a celestial body,
So that it shone fiercely with pride.
Her elegant fingers reached out and
Unravelled a thread of the galaxy,
With this she formed a circle bent at the edge.
Her tears fell and she mixed them with her love.
And she painted a sphere in resplendent colours as
Green as her eyes and as blue as her veins.
Then she danced, her carefree feet beat the
Rhythm of life.
As she looked down upon her globe, she felt
Poignancy, for she was alone and had no one,
So she plucked two hairs from her head and
Entwined her life into them, then set them upon the Earth.
She watched and beneath her solicitous gaze,
They grew and evolved.
Prayers floated up to her, but with no direction.
She took many of the sparkling diamonds,
And wove them, combined with her love and care,
Into a sphere, here she dwells, night after night,
Shining down rays of perfect silver,
Embodied with her love and protection.

Jessica Bull (12)
The Perse School For Girls